Assessing the Value

of the Medical Practice

Second Edition

John P. Reiboldt
The Coker Group

AMA press

Practice Success Series

Assessing the Value of the Medical Practice
Second Edition

Additional copies of this book may be ordered by calling 800 621-8335.
Secure on-line orders can be taken at www.amapress.com.
Mention product number OP315103.

ISBN 1-57947-406-3

BQ13:03-P-072:1/04

Library of Congress Cataloging-in-Publication Data

Reiboldt, John P.
  Assessing the value of the medical practice / John P. Reiboldt.—
2nd ed.
       p. ; cm.—(Practice success series)
"American Medical Association."
Rev. ed. of: Assessing the value of the medical practice / project
author, J. Max Reiboldt. c1996.
Includes bibliographical references and index.
  ISBN 1-57947-406-3
1. Medicine—Practice—Finance.
  [DNLM: 1. Practice Management, Medical. 2. Evaluation Studies.
3. Financial Management—methods. W 80 R3475a 2004] I. Reiboldt, J.
Max. Assessing the value of the medical practice. II. American Medical
Association. III. Title. IV. Series.
  R728.R455 2004
  610'.681—dc22
                                                    2003022229

The Coker Group, a leader in health care consulting, helps providers attain improved financial and operational results through sound business principles. The consulting team members are proficient, trustworthy professionals with experience and strengths in various areas. The well-rounded staff includes seasoned individuals in finance, administration, management, operations, compliance, personnel management, and information systems.

The Coker Group's nation-wide client base includes major health systems, hospitals, physician groups, and solo practitioners in a full spectrum of engagements. The Coker Group has gained a reputation since 1987 for thorough, efficient, and cost-conscious work to benefit its clients financially and operationally. The firm has a towering profile with recognized and respected health care professionals throughout the industry. Coker's exceptional consulting team has health care, technical, financial, and business knowledge and offers comprehensive programs, services, and training to yield long-term solutions and turnarounds. Coker staff members are devoted to delivering reliable answers and dependable options so that decision-makers can make categorical decisions. Coker consultants enable providers to concentrate on patient care.

Service Areas

- Practice management, billing and collection reviews, chart audits
- Procedural coding analysis
- Information systems review, including EMR
- Physician employment and compensation review
- Physician network development
- Practice appraisals
- Strategic planning/business planning
- Disengagements of practices and network unwinds
- Practice operational assessments
- Contract negotiations
- Hospital services, medical staff development
- Practice start-ups
- Buy/sell and equity analysis
- Sale/acquisition negotiations
- Group formation and dissolution
- Educational programs, workshops, and training
- Compliance plans
- HIPAA assessments and compliance

- MSA development
- Financial analysis
- Mediation and expert witnessing
- Policies and procedures manuals

For more information, contact:
The Coker Group
11660 Alpharetta Hwy, Suite 710
Roswell, GA 30076
800 345-5829
www.cokergroup.com

John P. Reiboldt, a senior consultant with The Coker Group, joined the firm in 1999. Mr Reiboldt's various projects for clients include pro forma financial statement analysis for start-up medical practices, financial analysis for medical entities, physician manpower plan, statistical analysis, practice appraisals, operational assessments, and medical staff surveys. Mr Reiboldt performs valuations, pro formas, and feasibility reviews for hospital-based clients and independent medical practices.

Mr Reiboldt has been published on several occasions, primarily in the *Journal of Medical Practice Management (JMPM)*. His article, "The Utility of Pro Forma Income Statements," September/October 2002, presents an artful case for the roles these oft-used tools play in financial management. Another article is underway for *JMPM* entitled "Seven Steps to Reducing Your Malpractice Liability." In addition to his work on this book on the process and craft of assessing the value of a medical practice, Mr Reiboldt contributed to a similar project on dermatology specialty-specific valuations for the American Academy of Dermatology.

Capitalizing in another area of expertise, Mr Reiboldt works with health systems and practicing physicians for the selection and implementation of practice management systems and electronic medical records, with the intention to assist in matching the appropriate software for the size and functions of the organization.

Mr Reiboldt is a graduate of the University of Mississippi, receiving an under-graduate degree in economics. He is currently an MBA candidate at Georgia State University.

Physicians want to know the value of their practices for a number of reasons. Some may be driven by career decisions (such as nearing retirement) or marketplace shifts and pressures. Others may be on the verge of offering partnership opportunities to younger or new associates. Likewise, those who are seeking partnership or ownership opportunities have reason to want to know true value. Other reasons may be of a more personal nature. Whatever the motive for determination, the question to ask is, "What is the real worth of the practice?"

Practice value is often difficult to assess, and the answer varies with the perception of who is asked. For instance, a physician has his or her own perspective because of the work invested throughout a number of years, usually an entire career. His or her spouse, attorney, accountant, or banker each may have a different point of view. None of these are likely to be totally objective.

Before entering into a practice valuation, the wisest practice owners or purchasers will want to know a great deal about the process of practice valuation and will engage a qualified appraiser to place a substantive figure on the practice's value. Ideally, the appraiser will be independent and impartial concerning the outcome of the analysis, basing his or her findings on quantifiable data and objective judgment and opinion. Subsequently, the valuation should determine a legitimate worth that can be used either for disposing of ownership or for basing an offer to acquire.

The purpose of this book is to inform the physician of the essential information for understanding the process of practice valuation so that he or she can engage a qualified practice appraiser and participate in the course of action. This book is by no means intended to instruct the physician on how to value a practice, but it is intended to give enough information so that the owner or purchaser can be assured that the work being done is based on recognized and respected valuation methods and valid information and resources.

Along with the description of valuation methods comes a wealth of resources that are available. These include extensive Internet resources and a glossary of terms so that the physician can feel comfortable with the language used by the appraiser throughout the valuation of the medical practice. As an owner of a medical practice, preparation should be taken prior to the valuation process in order to influence the outcome of the valuation. Such preparation includes setting in motion certain operational processes and management policies and procedures to ensure the ongoing stability of the practice. Again this should all be done prior to the valuation.

The intent of this book is to prepare the owner for what will transpire during a competent determination process, how to engage and work cooperatively with a qualified appraiser, and how to positively influence the outcome of the valuation.

7   Preparing the Practice for Maximum Value   87

chapter 1

Concepts of Value

Physicians, as a group, have various reasons for wanting to know the value of their medical practices. Those reasons can be chiefly dependent on current happenings in the industry or the physician's present career stage.

In past years, the well-accepted trend was for practice management companies, hospitals, and other entities to purchase physician practices as an effort to control the marketplace. The value of the practice had to be determined prior to the acquisition. Today, that notion has diminished substantially as fewer organizations are purchasing practices as a part of their marketing strategies. Furthermore, many physicians are deciding that they no longer wish to be part of the entities to which they sold their practices and are electing to disengage from them. The organizations that purchased the practices just a few years ago cannot simply "give" the practice back to the physician due to the current legal environment. Consequently, the physician must repurchase the practice to regain ownership, which calls for ascertaining a new value before the practice can change hands.

Selling the practice is not the only reason to have a valuation performed. A physician or entity may have a myriad of reasons for pursuing this information. Consider a practice that wishes to bring on a new partner. Likely, a new partner will need to make some type of investment in order to qualify for ownership. Without a valuation, the figure that represents the value of the practice would be nothing more than an arbitrary number picked out of the blue. However, everyone can be reasonably sure that the numbers are legitimate when they are derived from a fair and equitable valuation by a qualified, independent third party.

Finally, a valuation may be completed for no other reason than to assess the performance of a practice (ie, as management tools). How would an owner or group of owners measure the achievements or plight of their practice if they have nothing with which to compare it? Of course, numerous benchmarks can provide an excellent road map, but unless a detailed valuation is completed, it cannot be determined where the practice stands. Furthermore, because of the due diligence that must be thoroughly completed in order to calculate a value, certain operational issues may come to light that would have otherwise gone unnoticed. Thus, valuations can serve as excellent management tools.

REVENUE RULINGS

Understanding the theory behind the valuation process (as discussed in depth in Chapter 2) requires a good working knowledge of the various revenue rulings as determined by the Internal Revenue Service (IRS). IRS revenue rulings serve as the foundation for deriving a valuation of an entity. These revenue rulings—specifically Revenue Ruling 59-60—laid the foundation for virtually all that is discussed in this book and other books of this nature. Therefore, in order to understand the processes and methodologies of assessing the value of a medical practice, one must become familiar with the framework used to create those processes and methodologies.

IRS Revenue Ruling 59-60

Revenue Ruling 59-60 (RR 59-60) is often heralded as the most preeminent document regarding the valuation of a closely held entity. Whether intentional or unintentional, this document was years ahead of its time. RR 59-60 was originally drafted to provide guidance in estate and gift tax valuation purposes. However, throughout the years, it has become the predominant document used for determining valuation processes for all closely held entities.

In a period where both processes and methodologies are constantly being modified in order to keep pace with the changes in the business and regulatory environment, this time-tested document from the 1950s has remained constant in the realm of valuations and the valuation process. It has endured as the standard for more than half a century.

RR 59-60 sets a number of basic concepts and criteria that are still followed today throughout the valuation process. These factors establish the fundamental theory of business valuation, and each deserves diligent analysis and direct application in the valuing of an entity. The following is a brief list of some of the key components that must be considered as set by RR 59-60[1]:

- The nature of the business
- The history of the business from its start
- The economic outlook of the business
- The general condition and outlook of the industry
- The current financial condition of the business
- The earning capacity of the business
- The dividend paying capacity of the company
- The existence of goodwill or other intangible value
- The value of stock for sale or value of blocks of stock within the business
- Market prices of comparable business within the industry, whether stocks are actively traded in a free and open market or sold directly from business to business

While some of these factors are not applicable to the valuation of a medical practice, the appraiser must use a similar approach when valuing any other business. It is unimportant whether a practice is a sole proprietorship, a corporation, or a partnership; the value of the business relates to the business conducted and the historical and prospective financial performance of the entity.

Other Revenue Rulings

In addition to RR 59-60, a number of other rulings have greatly affected the manner in which closely held organizations are valued. While some of these may not directly affect the valuation methodologies of a closely held company, such as a solo medical practice, the preponderance of them contribute to the basic theory and assumptions that are utilized in the valuation process in general.

Some of the more important rulings that affect the valuation of a closely held company and their general contribution to the valuation process include the following:

- *Revenue Ruling 68-609 (RR 68-609).*   This ruling describes what is often referred to as the *formula method*, and it discusses the utilization of the formula approach in determining the fair market value of the intangible assets of a business **only** if there is no other suitable method for determining this value. The formula approach is also referred to as the *excess earnings method* (discussed in more depth in Chapter 3). Furthermore, the approach details the method in which the formula method should be based and considerations that should be made in using it, as well as providing language that supercedes Revenue Ruling 65-192 (RR 65-192).

- *Revenue Ruling 77-287 (RR 77-287).*   As noted in RR 77-287, "... The purpose of this ruling is to amplify Rev. Rul. 59-60 ... and to provide information and guidance to taxpayers, Internal Revenue Service personnel, and others concerned with the valuation, for Federal tax purposes, of securities that cannot immediately be resold because they are restricted from resale pursuant to Federal securities laws."[2]

- *Revenue Ruling 83-120 (RR 83-120).*   This ruling expounds on the valuation process and the factors that must be considered when valuing common and preferred stock. Where it goes into more depth in comparison to RR 59-60 is in the valuation of preferred stock and the unique considerations that it gains.

- *Revenue Ruling 93-1 (RR 93-1).*   This ruling specifically revokes Revenue Ruling 81-253 (RR 81-253) and addresses the issues of transferring ownership shares within a family and corporate control.

While none of these rulings specifically address the valuation of a closely held entity, per se, they form smaller parts of the whole that play a substantial role in the valuation processes and methodologies.

APPROACHES TO VALUE

Based on the aforementioned revenue rulings, the 3 major approaches to valuing a closely held company have been determined to be the market approach, asset-based approach, and the income approach.

While all of these approaches are based on contrastingly different methodologies, in theory, if performed correctly, they should conclude with the same valuation total. Of course, this is in theory; in actuality, the 3 different methodologies often draw varying conclusions.

Although Chapter 3 details each of the methodologies, a brief description of the 3 approaches is provided in the following sections.

Market Approach

The market approach is based on the theory of substitution and the underlying ". . . premise that a prudent buyer will pay no more for a property than it would cost to acquire a substitute property with the same utility."[3] This methodology applies comparative analysis of prices paid for similar assets or an entity in the marketplace. In this approach, the appraiser must estimate the value of the entity by applying data from similar companies, called guideline companies, to the same data from the subject company (ie, the company being valued).

While this market method must be completed in most cases, it, unfortunately, has little applicability to smaller practices. (In large part, this is due to the lack of data on these companies and their transactions.) However, with the onslaught of practice purchases and transitions occurring on a regular basis, information that can be applied will undoubtedly get better as time progresses. Currently, though, for valuation purposes of larger entities, the market approach is an integral portion of the valuation process.

Asset-based Approach

The asset-based approach is often referred to as the cost approach, the adjusted net asset approach, or the adjusted balance sheet approach. However, for the purposes of this analysis, the term *asset-based approach* will be used. This method, like that of the market approach, is based on the theory of substitution. However, while the market approach looks outward (ie, to other similar companies) for information to apply inward, the asset-based approach analyzes an entity's balance sheet and involves the individual valuation of each tangible and intangible asset residing on that entity's balance sheet.

In this approach, intangible assets—or a practice's goodwill—are valued using the excess earnings method. The downfall to this methodology is that if the business has more intangible value, the utilization of this approach becomes more difficult. Because of the increased intangible value (eg, RR 68-609), this methodology is often included as a supporting value and rarely used as the final value of an entity, especially in the case of a medical practice or other heavily service-oriented businesses.

Income Approach

The income approach is considered the closest to pure theory in which the fair market value of a company (discussed in Chapter 2) is the present value of all future benefits of the company. This methodology is the most widely used and accepted approach to the valuing of a closely held entity. Furthermore, it is best structured to determine the value of a medical practice.

However, as widely used and accepted as the income approach is, it is not faultless. In fact one of the major downfalls to this methodology is the fact that it is highly subjective in the underlying calculations used to reach a conclusive total, thus leaving room for mistakes and errors. If a highly skilled, competent appraiser is completing the process and is familiar with the method, this should play little role once a final value has been reached.

TANGIBLE AND INTANGIBLE ASSETS

An entity has 2 types of assets: tangible and intangible. Each type is discussed in the following sections.

Tangible Assets

An entity's tangible assets are generally the easiest to value because of their physical nature (ie, they can be touched, felt, and seen). This includes equipment, furniture, supplies, and fixtures. Because they are material, the appraiser can more easily associate a price to them. However, tangible assets also include those items that are not so easy to touch or see. These include items such as accounts receivable, cash, contracts, or notes receivable. While these items cannot be seen or held in a manner similar to a desk or an exam table, they are every bit as tangible and valuable.

These items are often confused and difficult to understand; therefore, following are definitions of the common tangible assets within a medical practice.

Equipment: All capital assets used to assist in the delivery of services within the physician practice. Such items include—but are certainly not limited to—lab equipment, diagnostic equipment, examining room equipment, procedure room equipment, etc.

Office supplies: While treated as an expense when purchased, most supplies are tangible assets when accumulated. Customarily, a physician's practice keeps a minimum of a one-month stock of office and medical supplies.

Office furniture: Tangible furniture includes desks, chairs, filing cabinets, etc.

Accounts receivable: Accounts receivable are those monies due from patients, insurance companies, and other creditors as a result of services provided within the practice.

Contracts of long-term (notes) receivables: These include contracts from long-term, income-generating projects within the practice.

Leasehold improvements: These are items added to the existing leased structure that may include plumbing, electrical, or other items of improvement. Typically, these items are permanently attached to the structure and are not removable when the lease ends.

Office building and land: The cost of the building and the land associated with the practice are tangible. Often, these are owned by separate entities and are leased back to the practice. Furthermore, if they are not directly part of the practice and its operations, these will warrant a separate real estate appraisal.

Cash and cash equivalents: This includes any cash on-hand within the practice's bank accounts, money market accounts, or any other extremely liquid vehicles. Cash equivalents are those items such as securities or other semi-liquid vehicles.

Automobiles: When owned by the practice, automobiles represent tangible value, and if they are to be included in the sale of the practice, then they should be treated as such.

Investments: This includes valid insurance policies and the market value of investments.

Leases: This may include any current capital leases entered into by the practice.

Intangible Assets

While tangible assets are those that can be seen, touched, and easily identified, intangible assets are just the opposite. They cannot be seen or touched and are often difficult to identify and value. Also, these are the most misunderstood aspects of the valuation of an entity. Intangible assets fall into 2 broad categories: *apart from goodwill* and *goodwill*.

Apart From Goodwill
Intangible value includes those assets that can be separated from the practice. They may include patient credit records, leasehold interests, trademarks, copyrights, patents, franchises, restrictive covenants, and the value of managed care contracting rights. Intangible assets can be separated from the practice because they have a definable cost basis and reasonable life expectancy separate from goodwill. If relevant, the appraiser considers the intangible value of these assets.

Goodwill
Goodwill is generally referred to as an intangible asset that cannot be separated from the practice. Unfortunately, this term causes confusion and remains difficult to explain. Even within the realms of experienced appraisers, this term evokes distinct variances of opinion and even controversies. However, the calculation of goodwill is most often the inherent value that we are trying to determine.

In larger organizations, such as those actively traded on public stock exchanges, goodwill is often referred to as the difference between the market value of the organization (ie, the total number of shares outstanding multiplied by the current price per share) less the tangible assets of the organization. Clearly, in a privately held entity, this would be difficult to determine due to the lack of a readily available price per share.

In some cases, companies would ". . . amortize goodwill, writing it off in relatively small, regular chunks each quarter over a period of years or decades until it was gone."[4] This commonly occurs in larger organizations such as hospitals, not in smaller physician practices.

However, with recent statements (Statements 141 and 142) from the Financial Accounting Standards Board (FASB), the method in which this goodwill is being carried on an entity's balance sheet has changed. Companies "can now keep goodwill on their balance sheets indefinitely. But they must perform annual tests to see if the goodwill has become 'impaired,' that is, if it has suffered a permanent decline in value. If it has, they must write off the entire impaired amount resulting in sometimes large"[4] changes in the amounts of goodwill the company can claim on its balance sheet. This goodwill and the treatment thereof is something that the appraiser must certainly consider.

Because it is the goal of the appraiser to value the goodwill of the entity, the appraiser must fully understand the concept of goodwill and how it applies to a company.

CONCLUSIONS

This chapter lays the groundwork for the in-depth review of the processes and methodologies that will follow. An appraiser must understand the theory and the basis for which the valuation is completed, and they must be knowledgeable of the foundation upon which these processes and methodologies have been constructed.

The completion of a valuation is much more than the entering of numbers into a formula in order to determine the value of an entity. While a valuation's roots are based in accounting, largely on accounting fundamentals, completing a valuation is less "black and white" and more related to theories and assumptions. Thus, an appraiser will often find that general certified public accountants (CPAs) with little or no experience in the valuation field have an extraordinarily difficult time in understanding the abstract thought that must be applied to the valuation process.

However, this is not to discount the necessity for being able to understand and competently navigate a corporation's financial statements, for without this, there will be no foundation in which to base the valuation theories.

Therefore, it is not the purpose of this book to teach the most basic financial operations because a thorough working knowledge of these issues must already be known. The intent of this book is to offer the additional knowledge and expertise needed to lay the groundwork for someone educated in these areas to perform a quality appraisal of a business entity.

NOTES

1. Internal Revenue Service. Revenue Ruling 59–60.
2. Internal Revenue Service. Revenue Ruling 77–287.
3. American Society of Appraisers. Introduction to Business Valuation, Part 1. In: *Principles of Valuation: Business Valuation Student Manual, BV 201.* Herndon, Va: American Society of Appraisers; 2002:7.
4. Casey EW, Wist B, et al. KPMG White Paper. *Accounting for Business Combinations, Goodwill, and Intangible Assets: An Analysis of FASB Statements 141 and 142.* KPMG LLP; 2001.

Valuation Process

Understanding the theory behind the valuation process allows one to understand the manner in which the valuation process should be completed. Completing the valuation process thoroughly and following the steps integral to this process will ensure that all relevant issues are addressed and resolved properly.

The American Society of Appraisers (ASA) has outlined the following 5 steps of the valuation process[1]:

1. Define the appraisal assignment
2. Gather the data
3. Analyze the data
4. Arrive at the valuation conclusion (ie, a value)
5. Write the report

Every valuation is unique and while similarities exist, it is not likely that any one valuation will be exactly the same. Generally, but not in all situations, the 5 steps will apply. The focus of this chapter is on the first step: define the appraisal assignment and draft the agreement.

DEFINE THE APPRAISAL ASSIGNMENT

The valuation process begins by defining the appraisal assignment, which is then incorporated into the letter of agreement stating and outlining the work that will be done. In developing a business valuation, an appraiser must identify and define the following valuation components:

- The basis of value (ie, business, business ownership interest, or security to be valued)
- The effective date of the appraisal (ie, the "as of" date)
- The standard of value (ie, what kind of value is desired)
- The purpose and the intended use of the valuation (somewhat similar to the standard of value)

The nature and scope of the assignment must be defined. Acceptable scopes of work will generally be 1 of 3 types: appraisal, limited appraisal, or calculations. Other scopes of work should be explained and described. These include the confidentiality agreement, statement of independence, statement of undue influence, medical records confidentiality agreement, and privacy statement.

Basis of Value

In order to determine the basis of value, the appraiser must ask, "What is going to be valued?" This question may seem elementary— for who would ask for a valuation when they do not even know what they want valued—but it is more complex. In fact, understanding what entity is going to be valued is fairly straightforward. If a physician wants the practice valued, then the appraiser will know to value the practice and everything that falls under the spectrum of the practice. The difficult part for the appraiser will be determining what portion of that entity will be valued.

In the case of a solo practitioner's practice, the practitioner may wish to only sell a portion of the practice. What if that portion equals a 75% interest? What if that portion equals only a 33% interest? For a large, multispecialty practice owned by a number of physicians, the appraiser must know implicitly what portion of this interest is being valued. The value of the whole may significantly differ from the value of a fraction, regardless of whether it is a large multispecialty practice or a solo practitioner's practice being valued.

As the ASA notes, "The different valuation approaches and methods used in a business appraisal produce different indications of value by the very nature of the empirical data used in the approach or method."[2]

The 3 bases of values that the appraiser must consider are *minority marketable*, *control*, and *minority nonmarketable* basis of value. The type of valuation that is completed will depend upon the basis that is considered.

When considered in the terms of completing a valuation, the idea of control and minority value are relatively easy to understand and the theory behind the basis of value is quite logical. First, consider the difference between a control and minority valuation. A *control valuation* is a valuation of a company, or portion thereof, which can be readily and easily affected by the owner of what is being valued. This will almost always be a private, or closely held company, because the ownership of this entity will have considerable control over the plight of that company.

Think of the instance where a large family practice clinic is being appraised. This practice started with one physician, and that physician has retained 100% of the ownership. That one physician has considerable control over the direction and management of the practice. If an individual was to purchase the ownership share of this practice, then this would be considered a control valuation. Thus, it is likely that the purchaser would pay a premium for the ability to have direct control over the business. Conversely, this ownership interest would have very little liquidity (ie, marketability) associated with it; as such, this lack of liquidity may call for a corresponding discount or decrease in value.

Now consider the opposite where a physician's practice was purchased by a publicly traded physician practice management company (PPMC) and in this purchase, the physician was granted an ownership portion of the PPMC. A number of other practices were bought as well, and these physicians were also made shareholders, totaling 1,000 physician-owners of the PPMC. If this physician chooses to sell his or her portion, this would be considered a minority basis of valuation because that one physician has very little control over the day-to-day decision-making process and his or her actions could not significantly affect the plight of the company. In this situation, an analyst would likely assert a discount to this minority stake. Though, as in the case of the control valuation where the ownership interest being valued was assumed to be relatively illiquid, which will most generally be the case, the minority share can be either highly liquid or highly illiquid. In the aforementioned example, the ownership portion would likely be very liquid, or marketable, meaning that it could easily and readily be transferred to another owner, like the ownership of stock in a public company. This is referred to as a minority marketable basis of value.

However, consider a similar example. Instead of a large group of physicians like the aforementioned example, this group consists of 4 providers and a minority share of 1 provider must be appraised. In this case, it may be more difficult to exchange or relinquish that individual's ownership share, thus rendering it less marketable. This would be considered a minority nonmarketable basis of valuation. A discount for both minority ownership and lack of marketability may be considered.

As pointed out in the examples in this section, it is evident that an appraiser must be aware of the entity that is being valued in order to properly conduct the valuation.

Standard of Value

The next step in the valuation process is determining what kind of value is wanted. This will largely be determined by the answer to another question: What is the purpose of this valuation? The answers to these 2 key questions must be addressed before progress can be made.

As noted in Chapter 1, valuations are not completed only when someone wants to buy or sell an entity or a portion of an entity. There are numerous reasons as to why an entity may require a valuation, including the transfer of ownership (ie, buying or selling) of a company. A few of the more common reasons for conducting a valuation include the following:

- Buying or selling
- Tax related
- Financial reporting
- Legal issues
  — Divorce
  — Damages, etc
- Internal issues
  — Buy/sell agreements
  — Stock distributions
  — Adding/disengaging a partner

While there are numerous reasons why an appraisal must be performed, the end use of the appraisal must be clear in order to determine the appropriate standard of valuation.

Fair Market Valuation

Fair market valuation is defined in IRS RR 59-60 as, ". . . [T]he amount at which the property would change hands between a willing buyer and a willing seller, when the former is not under any compulsion to buy and the latter is not under any compulsion to sell; both parties having reasonable knowledge of relevant facts."[3] The 5 characteristics of a market value are as follows[4]:

1. The buyer and seller are typically motivated.
2. Both parties are well-informed or well-advised and acting in what they consider their best interests.
3. A reasonable time is allowed for exposure in the open market.
4. Payment is made in terms of cash or financial arrangements comparable thereto.
5. The price represents the normal consideration for the property sold unaffected by special or creative financing or sales concessions granted by anyone associated with the sale.

Although the terms *market value* and *cash value* are used interchangeably, *fair market value* is not to be confused with *fair value*.

Fair Value

The term *fair value* can be used in 2 different instances: legal and financial. Fair value for legal purposes is usually that which is determined by a court of law, and it does not have to be associated with fair market value. This value and the calculation that results usually vary based on state laws and regulations and bear little resemblance to fair market value. Furthermore, due to its various meanings, there is little uniformity in the definition of fair legal value. In cases of fair legal value, there does not have to be a willing buyer or seller. These are most often used in cases of shareholder dissent or minority oppression cases. Fair value in regards to financial reporting is more strongly associated with tax and generally accepted accounting principles than with valuation terms.

Investment Value

Investment value is the specific value of goods or services to a particular investor (or class of investors) based on individual investment requirements and expectation. The investment value often calculates a different value than the fair market value. In determining fair market value, the buyer and seller are equals; however, when calculating the investment value of an entity, 1 side of the equation (ie, the buyer or the seller) may have significantly different reasons for wanting to make such an investment. No specific reason exists for why an entity may be of more value to one particular owner than to another; in fact, there may be a myriad of reasons.

The basic premise behind the determination of investment value is the assumptions used to determine this value. When determining investment value over fair market value, the assumptions will generally be skewed to meet the predetermined standards set by the investor.

Intrinsic Value

Intrinsic value is often referred to as *fundamental value.* This "represents an analytical judgment of value based on the perceived characteristics inherent in the investment, not tempered by characteristics peculiar to one investor, but rather tempered by how these perceived characteristics are interpreted by one analyst versus another."[5] This is basically a fancy way of saying intrinsic value is fair market value with the variances caused by the market (ie, supply and demand) removed.

Intrinsic value is often used in stock analysis of a company. For instance, the statement may be that "The stock price has been lowered, but its fundamentals still look good." This means that the supply or demand for the stock has caused it to lose value, but the actual value of the stock remains sound. So for a publicly traded stock in the market, a stock analyst would likely consider this devalued stock a "buy."

Purpose for Valuation

The next step in the valuation process is determining the purpose for the valuation. The purpose for valuation and the standard of value are similar to the "chicken and egg" conundrum (ie, which one came first; to know one, the other must also be known). The various purposes for valuating an entity lead to different ways to determine the standard of value that will be used.

An entity may consider completing a valuation for numerous reasons. The most obvious reason for performing a valuation is to determine the value of an entity for the purpose of buying or selling it. Another reason may be for tax purposes, so that tax implications (eg, IRS assessed excise or estate taxes) can be determined.

Yet another reason for completing a valuation is for legal purposes. When determining the value for legal reasons, the court will often specify a fair value, not fair market value. Legal purposes are most often used in divorce or dissenting shareholder cases, although value may be determined for other reasons. Legal purposes can also be used to assess damages to one party or for partnership dissolutions. While the reasons can be varying, as the name implies these valuations can often be burdened by legal and other complexities, making some appraisers somewhat reluctant to assume these types of projects.

Probably the most common reason for determining the value of an entity or a portion thereof is for internal reasons. This may be for financial reporting, buy/sell agreements, stock distributions, adding/leaving partner, or for a number of other purposes. Determining the valuation for internal purposes is particularly important for closely held companies. In this case the shareholders do not have the luxury of finding out their current stock value just by looking on the Internet as would the owner of a publicly held company. Instead, these physicians must determine the value of their company based on an appraisal. Most bylaws of closely held companies will call for the determination of fair market value to be completed on an annual basis, if not biannually.

Also, buy/sell agreements will often call for an updated valuation to be completed when a new shareholder is added. While these will often be limited as to when they can be executed to correspond with the prearranged valuation, if they are not, it is certainly both in the interest of the current shareholders and the new shareholder to know the value of the stock when purchasing it.

Closely held companies will often include a valuation of their company with the annual financial statements. The price of a company's stock is a great barometer for determining the performance of the company, and without the benefit of easily being able to find this out (ie, through public information), a valuation often serves as an excellent supplement to a company's annual financial documents.

One can see how an appraiser must know what they are valuing in order to establish the standard of value that will be used. If an appraiser has been contracted by an individual who seeks to purchase a medical practice in a particular city or area of the country, that individual may be willing to pay a little more than a practice's fair market value to get what they want. For this reason, the appropriate standard for valuation in this case would likely be investment value. However, if a board of directors wanted to see how their company's value had increased since the last year, they may be more interested in intrinsic value rather than fair market value.

Before the valuation process can begin, the appraiser *must* know why this valuation is being completed. This will serve as the foundation for all of the assumptions made in calculating the value.

TYPE OF APPRAISAL

This section describes what is necessary to complete an appraisal of a medical entity. It should be noted, however, that a full appraisal is not always what is needed or required by the client.

Often times a potential client will contact an appraiser, asking for a valuation of a specific entity but not a full valuation. For example, when a physician wishes to buy into a practice and the physician-owners offer a buy-in price, the prospective partner will want to validate that number. In this case, the prospective partner may choose to hire an appraiser to determine if the asking price is a valid number that falls within the realm of reasonableness. The prospective partner may ask for a limited appraisal just to "run the numbers" and determine if the offer is within reason.

Another example of why an appraisal might be conducted is when an entity wants to know the company's value based on the prospect of certain events or changes in the company. This would be considered a *pro forma* or *hypothetical valuation*.

While these initiatives vary significantly from a full valuation, there is nothing that makes completing these appraisals unethical to the appraiser. However, the appraiser must make it known that this is what the client has asked him or her do, and that this is all he or she are doing. This must be stated clearly and be understood by both parties before an agreement to complete a valuation is executed.

Appraisal

"The objective of an appraisal is to express an unambiguous opinion about the value of the business . . . which is supported by all procedures that the appraiser deems to be relevant to the valuation."[6] An appraisal is a valuation that considers all aspects of the business and considers—but does not necessarily apply—all methods of valuation (ie, income, market, asset-based) in order to determine the value of an entity.

An appraisal will clearly state the conclusions of the appraisal analysis (ie, the value of the entity) based on all relevant information as of the appraisal date. The conclusion, or value, can be stated based on a defined, exact figure, or it can be expressed as a range. Whichever way the value is expressed must be clearly agreed upon between the appraiser and the client. In addition to the conclusion, the information used to calculate the appraisal conclusion will be outlined in detail. The procedures and methodology used to collect, analyze, and reach the conclusion will also be outlined. Finally, an appraisal will *consider* all of the approaches to valuation.

Notice the emphasis on consider in the previous sentence. Even though all of the approaches to value must be *considered*, this does not mean that the appraiser must apply all of the approaches. It is the discretion of the appraiser to apply the most appropriate approach.

For example, a physician's office will likely have very few assets (ie, tangible, intangible), so it *may* not be appropriate to apply the asset-based approach to value. Whether or not an approach is to be applied, as has been stated, is the sole discretion of the appraiser, though, the choice to include or exclude a particular approach to value must be an educated decision, not just the analyst's decision to disregard one particular approach. If the analyst chooses not to apply one approach, the reasoning for doing so must be fully defendable.

Limited Appraisal

The limited appraisal is very similar to an appraisal; however, due to the differences, the appraiser is required to note that the calculations that have been used are limited in nature. This is usually (though not always) necessary due to the fact that the appraiser has not been given access to all the data needed to complete an appraisal.

A limited appraisal will fully document the value of the entity (as either an exact amount or a range) with all 3 approaches to value being considered by the appraiser. The differences between the limited appraisal and the appraisal are in the information gathering, research, and analysis of the valuation process (often referred to as *due diligence*) in that the appraiser has based the valuation conclusions on limited relevant information, or completed only a limited due diligence process. Regardless of why or which process has been limited in nature, all processes needed to complete an appraisal have not been met. The outcome, therefore, will be a limited appraisal.

Because an appraisal is limited in nature does not mean that it is not "right." In fact, it may be the desire of the client to have a limited appraisal completed, though, this should be clearly defined in the letter of engagement and agreed upon by the appraiser and the client. In addition, the fact that this appraisal is limited in nature should be clearly stated in the report. The worse thing that could happen between an appraiser and a client is if the client thinks that he or she has an appraisal while the appraiser has only completed a limited appraisal. In such a case, both individuals will likely walk away from the appraisal with embarrassment.

Calculations

A *calculation* expresses the value of an entity (either as 1 figure or a range of figures). It is similar to the limited appraisal in the fact that it can be based on limited data and a limited data-collection process. It differs in its approach to value. In the case of the calculation, the appraiser and the client will usually agree upon the type of approach to value that will be used prior to the appraisal.

Typically, an analysis on this level will be for the client and used for informational purposes. For example, a client may request that an appraiser value his or her entity based only on a financial analysis (ie, no review of operations, thus limiting the due diligence that has been dedicated to this assignment) and using the income approach. This approach could be chosen because this was used 5 years ago when the practice was valued and the owner wants to see, based strictly on a financial review, if the value of the practice has appreciated or declined.

Again, a valuation for this purpose can be completed, though, it must be expressly agreed upon by the client and defined by the appraiser within the report.

Hypothetical Appraisal

Appraisals, limited appraisals, and calculations are based upon reasonable assumptions that best resemble the future operations of the entity being valued. However, the client may choose not to see the value of the entity under the most reasonable assumptions for future operations, but instead under assumptions as to "potential" future operations, or pro forma.

A client may wish to see what the value of the practice will be if staff increases productivity by 50% rather than the likely growth rate of 10%. Or the client may choose to see the value if the provider compensation decreased rather than increased by 5% per year. These are examples of hypothetical scenarios (ie, scenarios that do not coincide with projected future operations as determined by the appraiser) used to calculate the value of an entity.

Often, a client will request that an appraiser complete an appraisal of the entity, and in addition to the appraisal, determine what will happen to the value if other scenarios are applied. A hypothetical appraisal can be an appraisal, a limited appraisal, or just based on calculations. These are often useful planning tools for the client, though regardless of their intended use, it must be fully documented that they are hypothetical. If an appraiser is acting as an independent analyst and basing the calculations on his or her own independently formulated assumptions, it is very important to note that the appraisal is hypothetical due to the fact that most hypothetical appraisals are based on assumptions dictated by the client or a representative of the client. Thus, failure to note that the appraisal is hypothetical could drastically impugn the independence of the appraiser.

LETTER OF ENGAGEMENT

Before any valuation work can be completed, the client requiring the valuation must request the services of a valuation professional. This is typically memorialized in a *request for services letter* or *letter of engagement* between the professional (ie, usually the firm that employs the appraiser) and the client.

This letter of engagement should be thorough in its scope, expressly defining all of the details of the potential project. This is a very important letter because it lays the foundation for the future project.

Generally, and certainly depending on the size and scope of the valuation that will be completed, the letter of engagement will go through a number of changes and modifications in order to properly define all that is necessary to complete the project. Reasons for this may vary, but these changes and modifications take place so that the project can be properly defined based on the desires of the client.

On larger projects, the drafting of the letter of engagement will typically be the result of numerous meetings—both on-site and off-site—between the client and the appraiser. These meetings will allow the professional to better define that which the client desires to be completed. Thus, because the appraiser and the client have been able to discuss the loads of minutiae contained (and required) in the letter of engagement, it is less likely that the letter of engagement will require as many, if any, modifications.

Nevertheless, in the case of a smaller client, the letter of engagement may only be the result of a single telephone call or brief meeting. In such cases the appraiser may have limited information about what the client needs, or simply may have misinterpreted what the client needs, thus, changes and modifications may be required. There is nothing wrong or unethical about making changes or modifications to the letter of engagement; however, making changes to the letter of engagement *after* the agreement has been consummated is highly unprofessional and should never occur. Revisions before signing the agreement are virtually always required because once the letter of engagement has been executed by all of the necessary parties, it shall stand as a legally binding and enforceable contract. Any breach should be regarded as a breach of contract.

It is understandable that issues will arise that will potentially change that which has been defined in the letter of engagement. In such cases it may be necessary to supplement or update the original letter of engagement, again, expressly outlining the details involved, the reason for the changes, and agreement by all parties involved.

Figure 2-1 is an example of a letter of engagement for a medium-sized medical practice. This figure contains all of the necessary information that must be agreed upon by the client and the appraiser, such as the basis of value, the standard of value that will be applied,

FIGURE 2-1
Letter of Engagement

Healthcare Appraisers, LLC (the "Appraiser"), is pleased to present *Atlanta Orthopedic Physicians, PA* (the "Client"), the practice of John D. Smith, MD, and Bob A. Jones, MD (the "Physicians"), with this Letter of Engagement ("Letter") to outline the Appraiser's proposed approach to the completion of the Valuation and Assessment ("Valuation") of *South Atlanta Orthopedics and Physical Therapy, LLC* (the "Practice"). This Letter shall consist of Appraiser's:

■ Understanding of the issues

■ Proposed method of completion

■ Summary of fees

Understanding of the Issues

Appraiser understands that the Client wishes to purchase the controlling (one-hundred percent) ownership interest of the Practice in the South Atlanta area. The Client is requesting that Appraiser complete a valuation and assessment, as defined below, of the Practice in order to determine a price that may be offered to the Practice by the Client.

Proposed Method of Completion

Appraiser has divided the proposed method of completion into two categories: Project I and Project II. Both of these Projects comprise the detailed Valuation of the Practice. They are defined as follows:

Project I: Practice Valuation and Limited Assessment

Project I shall consist of a detailed valuation and limited operational assessment of the Practice. This review shall encompass the ongoing operations and associated revenue generated by the Practice. This includes a review of its current operations, with special emphasis on its historical performance trends and overall estimates of future performance. This review will include a limited operational assessment that will allow Appraiser to gain a better perspective of the Practice's financial operations.

The intent of this review is to determine the fair market value of the Practice via a full appraisal. The independently derived value will serve as the standard for determining the potential sale/acquisition price of the Practice and will be proposed as a single dollar figure. The completion of this process is independent—that is, without influence from either side (ie, the Client and the Practice)—however, it shall be completed on behalf of the Client.

Phase One

Initial Assessment and Review of Information Off-site. Appraiser will commence its review of the Practice by submitting a checklist of information. Upon submission, Appraiser will review this in preparation of on-site work.

Professional Fees

Estimated hours to complete this phase:
      x to x hours @ $xxx per hour $xxx to $xxx

Phase Two

On-site Review. Appraiser will conduct an on-site review of the Practice encompassing analysis of operations in the context of the definition of this assignment review. Appraiser will complete this work by meeting with the physician/owner and other appropriate representatives of the practice and reviewing all key areas inherent to the scope of this assignment. From the work completed during this on-site review, Appraiser will then be prepared to complete the actual independent Valuation report within the context of this assignment.

Professional Fees

Estimated hours to complete this phase:
      x to x days on-site @ $xxx per day* (one consultant) $xxx to $xxx

Phase Three

Formal Report. After completing Phases One and Two, Appraiser will be prepared to complete the formal report, indicating the valuation conclusions. Furthermore, this report will include a limited operational assessment of the Practice as noted above. This phase will include the compilation and submission of that formal report documenting this information.

Professional Fees

Estimated hours to complete this phase:

  x to x hours @ $xxx per hour $xxx to $xxx

Project II: Detailed Operational Assessment

Project II shall consist of a detailed operational assessment in addition to the valuation report described in Project I. This will be completed in the place of the limited operational assessment as described in Project I and will encompass an in-depth review of all issues of the Practice. Appraiser will perform this assessment via an on-site review and will summarize—in detail—the findings of the analysis. Furthermore, Appraiser will summarize those areas of operations currently being completed in the Practice and identify any improvements that could be made and suggest any corrective action regarding the current operations.

The detailed assessment will include, but is not limited to, a review of the following operational areas:

- Personnel review
  - —Hours worked
  - —Pay scale
  - —Benefits
  - —Competence level
  - —Management structure
  - —Duties and job responsibilities
- Revenue cycle analyses (including billing/collections functions)
- Internal controls and procedures
- Management information/practice operating systems review
- Scheduling procedures
- Patient management/patient flow procedures
- Regulatory compliance
- Lease reviews
  - —Facility leases
  - —Capital leases
  - —Employee leases
  - —Equipment leases
- Expense structure
- Financial performance (historical and prospectively)
- Demographic analysis
  - —Current patients' payer analysis
  - —Current patients' age analysis
  - —Current patients' zip code analysis

Professional Fees

Estimated hours to complete this phase:

    x to x hours @ $xxx per hour (one consultant) $xxx to $xxx

* These hours/fees are in addition to Project I, Phase III hours/fees.

Continued

FIGURE 2-1

Letter of Engagement—*Continued*

Summary of Fees

Project I: Practice Valuation and Limited Assessment

Phase One:	Off-site preparation	$xxx to $xxx
	(x to x hours @ $xxx per hour)	
Phase Two:	On-site review	$xxx to $xxx
	(x to x days on-site @ $xxx per day)	
Phase Three:	Formal report	$xxx to $xxx
	(x to x hours @ $xxx per hour)	

Total fees for Project I   **$xxx to $xxx**

Project II: Detailed Operational Assessment

Formal Report
(x to x hours @ $xxx per hour) $xxx to $xxx

Total fees for Project II (*in addition to Project I fees*)   **$xxx to $xxx**

Total Fees, Projects I and II   **$X,XXX to $X,XXX**

Subsequent to completing the above phases, further needed analysis and assistance in the negotiation and the purchase/sale process as well as any other updates to the valuation, including changes of assumptions, etc, will be subject to additional professional fees. Unless agreed otherwise, Appraiser's fee of $xxx to $xxx per hour will prevail, depending upon the consultant's experience level. All work will be documented and substantiated by Appraiser, submitted to the Client.

An initial billing of $xxx toward the completion of this assignment will result at the execution of this Agreement. The remainder will be billed after the completion of each project. The Client will remit payment to Appraiser within 10 days of invoicing.

The Client will also reimburse Appraiser for its travel and out-of-pocket expenses incurred by its consultant(s) during this project. Appraiser will submit proper documentation to support these expenses. Such charges include, but are not limited to, airfare, lodging, meals, rental car, parking, etc, while on-site. Overnight shipping expenses will be reimbursed to Appraiser within thirty (30) days of billing.

Execution below indicates agreement to Appraiser to pursue the below-noted projects associated with the preparation and completion of this assignment.

Project(s) to Complete   (By initialing, you signify your decision to complete the project.)

Project I: _____

Project II: _____

FOR ATLANTA ORTHOPEDIC PHYSICIANS, PA

_____   _____
John D. Smith, MD   Date

_____   _____
Bob A. Jones, MD   Date

FOR HEALTHCARE APPRAISERS, LLC

_____   _____
Consultant   Date

The referenced practice and physician names in this and the following figures are, to the best of the author's knowledge, fictitious and not true practices/providers.

the type of appraisal, the purpose of the appraisal, who will be completing the appraisal, when it will be completed, the type of value that will be provided (ie, an exact figure or a range), the fees that will be charged to the client, and more.

As previously noted, in order to complete a full appraisal, the analyst must fully understand the operations of the entity that will be valued; thus the analyst must complete a review of not only the entity's financials, but also of its basic operations (eg, management, daily operations, long-term planning). Because this must be completed, the client has an excellent opportunity to complete both a detailed valuation and assessment of the entity's operations. This review is often more involved than a typical appraisal and will take more of the analyst's time, thereby increasing the cost to the client. In addition, the professional completing the valuation must not only be knowledgeable in the field of valuations but also in the field of business that is in question, specifically medical practice management and operations.

Someone not intimate with the operations of a medical practice or a hospital, for example, would certainly be able to complete the financial valuation based on their knowledge as an appraiser, but without a thorough understanding of operations of these entities, it is highly unlikely that they would be able to perform a detailed assessment. This is why, especially in the field of medical practice, it is beneficial to procure a valuation professional with a detailed working knowledge of the field in which they are valuing and why such a professional can often add that additional knowledge that another professional who is less familiar with practice operations may not bring to the table.

Other Agreements

The appraiser may choose to incorporate these other agreements into the letter of engagement or may provide them as separate documents, as they are presented here. These are documents that provide additional support and representation for the client to the appraiser and vice versa and add a supplementary level of understanding. These documents include the following:

- *Confidentiality agreement.* This letter maintains that anything that is discussed between the client and the appraiser will remain confidential at all times, before, during, and after the valuation process. Although confidentiality is expected, this agreement further documents the understanding between the 2 parties. Figure 2-2 is an example of a confidentiality agreement.
- *Statement of independence.* The purpose of this statement is to ensure that the appraiser and the client and any other third parties shall remain independent at all times. Again, this should go without saying; however, an official statement documenting the fact that the appraiser shall remain independent throughout this process and that no party shall attempt to impugn the appraiser's independence is necessary. Figure 2-3 is an example of a statement of independence.

FIGURE 2-2

Confidentiality Agreement

Atlanta Orthopedic Physicians, PA, of Atlanta, Georgia, (the "Client") has agreed to engage *Healthcare Appraisers, LLC* (the "Appraiser") to perform a valuation and assessment of the operations of *South Atlanta Physical Therapy, LLC* (the "Practice").

The Client, Practice, and Appraiser acknowledge the sensitive and confidential nature of the information to be disclosed, and acknowledge the importance of the continued confidentiality of such information.

In consideration for consent to disclose this information, Appraiser agrees and covenants that it will not at any time, directly or indirectly, disclose or communicate to any person, firm, or corporation, in any manner whatsoever, any information disclosed to Appraiser without the express written consent of the Practice, understanding the report will go directly to the Practice and be available for its review and internal use.

FOR ATLANTA ORTHOPEDIC PHYSICIANS, PA

_____   _____

                                                    Date

FOR SOUTH ATLANTA PHYSICAL THERAPY, LLC

_____   _____

                                                    Date

FOR HEALTHCARE APPRAISERS, LLC

_____   _____

Consultant   Date

FIGURE 2-3

Statement of Independence

Healthcare Appraisers, LLC (the "Appraiser") acknowledges that as the selected professional to perform the valuation and assessment of *South Atlanta Physical Therapy, LLC* (the "Practice"), it will perform its work with total independence and in no way will the value of the Practice be influenced by the entity that will pay the appraiser's professional fees (ie, the "Client").

Furthermore, Appraiser certifies that to the best of its knowledge, there exists no known conflicts of interest that would cause or even illicit the perception of a lack of independence pertaining to the valuation of the Practice.

FOR HEALTHCARE APPRAISERS, LLC

_____   _____

Consultant   Date

■ *Statement of undue influence.* Another statement that should support that which should hold true in any situation is the statement of undue influence. This statement documents the fact that the professional will not be influenced by any party and serves as proof for the appraiser's professionalism. Figure 2-4 provides an example that is not an agreement between all parties but rather a statement being made by the appraiser.

FIGURE 2-4

Statement of Undue Influence

> *Atlanta Orthopedic Physicians, PA* (the "Client") has requested that *Healthcare Appraisers, LLC* (the "Appraiser") complete a valuation and assessment of *South Atlanta Physical Therapy, LLC* (the "Practice"). The Client acknowledges that Appraiser will function in total independence and therefore will not exert undue influence to in any way affect the findings and Appraiser's recommendations. The fee for this work will in no way be contingent upon the valuation total derived or the conclusions derived therein.
>
> **FOR ATLANTA ORTHOPEDIC PHYSICIANS, PA**
>
> _____   _____
>   Date
>
> **FOR HEALTHCARE APPRAISERS, LLC**
>
> _____   _____
> Consultant   Date

- *Medical records confidentiality agreement.* When valuing a medical practice, an appraiser must consider the patients' medical records. This information is highly confidential and should be treated as such. This is why it is appropriate to produce a confidentiality agreement noting the purpose for the appraiser examining the records, the limit on information that will be taken from each record, and the fact that the appraiser has received permission by the appropriate individuals to review these confidential documents. When an appraiser is to take note of such important and confidential data, it is beneficial to all parties involved that a statement of confidentiality be executed (see Figure 2-5).
- *Privacy statement.* Every appraisal (and consultative) firm should have a statement documenting its privacy clause and the limits of its liability in regards to the privacy it provides to the client (and other third parties) and information pertaining to the client (and other third parties).

Appraisal Fee

The fee for the appraisal is one of the most important facets of the engagement both to the client and to the appraiser: to the appraiser because this serves as the method in which the respective firm will generate its revenues, and to the client because this will be the fund into which the client is responsible to pay for the services provided.

Often, the appraiser and the client have differing perspectives on appropriate professional fees. This is why it is imperative for the appraiser to outline the fees, terms of payment, and method of calculation.

Typically, a professional firm's fees are calculated and charged to the client by an hourly rate, and for each incremental time period (ie, either every quarter-hour, half-hour, or other fraction) of work provided. While larger firms and larger clients may be more amenable

FIGURE 2-5

Medical Records Confidentiality Agreement

Atlanta Orthopedic Physicians, PA, of Atlanta, Georgia, (the "Practice") has agreed to engage *Healthcare Appraisers, LLC,* to perform a valuation and assessment of the operations of *South Atlanta Physical Therapy, LLC* (the "Practice").

The Client, Practice, and Appraiser acknowledge the sensitive and confidential nature of the information provided within medical records and the importance of such information. In consideration for consent to disclose this information, Appraiser agrees and covenants that it will not at any time, directly or indirectly, disclose or communicate to any person, firm, or corporation, in any manner whatsoever, a patient's name or in any way jeopardize the privacy between the provider/physician and the patient. It is understood, however, that this review may encompass specific recommendations for improvements needed in documentation, adherence to risk management protocols, including proper chart organization, all of which will be done within the context and purpose of Appraiser's review.

FOR ATLANTA ORTHOPEDIC PHYSICIANS, PA

_____   _____

                                                                              Date

FOR SOUTH ATLANTA PHYSICAL THERAPY, LLC

_____   _____

                                                                              Date

FOR HEALTHCARE APPRAISERS, LLC

_____   _____

Consultant   Date

to such a fee structure, smaller practices/clients are typically very cost-conscience and tend to shy away from such fee structures. In these cases, it may be appropriate (see Figure 2-1) for the appraiser to base fees on an hourly basis, yet cap the total fees of the project. This will ensure the client that the charges will not exceed those quoted in the letter of engagement.

However, the appraiser must be very careful when quoting hourly based, capped fees because if the project becomes too extensive and requires more work than originally assumed to produce a suitable valuation, then the appraiser will likely absorb the cost of those additional hours that cannot be billed. Also, the client may begin to request that additional work be completed or try to take advantage of the appraiser for work not included in the scope of the original letter of engagement. Thus, the appraiser should always include in the letter of engagement specific wording on what the valuation entails, and anything over and above that, or if information is brought to light that considerably changes the time that the appraiser must contribute should be subject to additional fees. It may be difficult to distinguish what is and what is not a part of the original assignment; thus, it is beneficial to discuss this with the client before work begins.

Another method in which the appraiser may generate fees is to set a flat fee that the client is charged. While the client may favor this method, it often puts the burden of completing the project under the set fees on the appraiser. This cost structure may be suitable for smaller projects (eg, the case where a client chooses to run a brief hypothetical valuation for internal analytical purposes); it is not generally the best method for larger, more substantial projects.

All of the previously stated methods are suitable for basing the professional fees for a project; however, some methods of basing fees are not appropriate. Most notably is the method of basing professional fees on a percentage of actual value. This not only puts the client at a disadvantage, but it could also potentially impugn the independence and unduly influence the judgment of the appraiser by raising the valuation conclusion to increase the fees that are due. It is important for the appraiser to note that the fees from the project are not based on the conclusion as calculated in the appraisal. (Appraisal fees are discussed in more detail in Chapter 4.)

CONCLUSION

This chapter addresses many important steps of assessing the value of a health care entity that must be defined before the appraisal can be completed. From the issue of what will be valued, to how it will be valued, to the details of the agreement and the establishment of fees, each aspect affects the integrity of the whole process. If the assignment is more precisely defined, the better the client's valuation.

NOTES

1. American Society of Appraisers. Introduction to Business Valuation, Part 1. In: *Principles of Valuation: Business Valuation Student Manual, BV 201.* Herndon, Va: American Society of Appraisers; 2002:26–27.

2. Ibid., 14.

3. Internal Revenue Service. Revenue Ruling 59–60.

4. Pratt S, Reilly R, Schweihs R. *Valuing a Business: The Analysis and Appraisal of Closely Held Companies.* 4th ed. New York, NY: McGraw-Hill; 2000.

5. Ibid., 31.

6. American Society of Appraisers. General Requirements for Developing a Business Valuation. In: *Business Valuation Standards, BVS-I.* Herndon, Va: American Society of Appraisers; 2001.

chapter 3

Valuation Methods

Now that the foundation for the appraisal and valuation process has been explained, the various methodologies used for calculating the value of a health care entity (eg, a medical practice, ambulatory surgical center, business units that deliver health care) will be examined. Thus far, the 3 basic concepts of value have been defined as the following:

- Market approach
- Asset-based approach
- Income approach

All 3 approaches are acceptable to use in the appraisal process. Furthermore, Chapter 1 discussed the concept of tangible and intangible value and how these relate to the 3 approaches. In this chapter, each approach will be examined and reviewed in detail. (It should be noted that all figures in Chapter 3 are based on the financial statements found in the Appendix A.)

MARKET APPROACH

The market approach uses comparative analysis of prices paid for similar assets or entities in the marketplace. "This approach is based on the principle of substitution premise in that a buyer will pay no more for property than it would cost to acquire a substitute property with the same utility."[1] While the process is completely different, this is similar to the method used to value real estate, whereas, the entity being valued (eg, the facility, house) is compared to other, similar entities (eg, facilities, buildings).

Choosing the Market Methodology

In this process, the appraiser uses guideline companies, or similar companies, to derive multiples that are then applied to data from the health care entity or medical practice (ie, subject company) under consideration. Do not confuse, though, the term *guideline companies* with *comparable companies* because rarely are 2—much less 3 or 4— entities so much alike that they can be considered comparable. In fact, Revenue Ruling 59-60 (RR 59-60) defines the companies that should be used as *similar*.

Once it has been determined that the market approach is applicable to the valuation of the subject company and the basis of valuation is known, appropriate guideline companies should be chosen.

Data from guideline companies are available from the stock market, or publicly traded companies (see Figure 3-1).

Unfortunately, this information is usually more applicable to the value of minority-marketable subject companies (see Chapter 2) because they have little power to make a decision and are marketable and very liquid (ie, easy to sell). Minority-marketable subject companies are just like the value from shares of a public company's stock (eg, General Electric), in that the owner of one share of a public company stock has little power to make a decision for the whole company. In these companies, even the largest institutional investor will not generally own more than 5% of a company; ownership can be easily and readily sold or transferred. If this is not the basis of valuation that will be performed, other sources of information must be found or adjustments made to the guideline company's information to more resemble this type of company. This method of valuing an entity is often referred to as the *market multiple method*.

Another good source of guideline data is from companies that have been acquired by other companies or that have completed an initial public offering (IPO) for its stock. In this case, the guideline company's stock is, or is very near, a control-marketable value (see Chapter 2), which would likely be more beneficial to the analysis, though, some considerations or adjustments may still need to be made.

This method considers other transactions that have occurred in the marketplace and uses those transactions to derive various multiples that will be used (as in the market multiple method) to place a

FIGURE 3-1

Public Company Method

Public Company	As Of	Price Per Share	Revenue	EBITDA	Shares Outstanding	Market Capitalization	Invested Capital
NPT	12/31/2003	$22.75	$102,325,455	$19,568,467	100,555,232	$2,287,631,528.00	$105,858,632
PTA	12/31/2003	$7.58	$77,258,952	$7,035,111	13,585,653	$102,979,249.74	$102,589,325
OA	12/31/2003	$9.81	$45,895,235	$8,987,025	15,252,222	$149,624,297.82	$32,577,789
NO	4/30/2003	$32.55	$195,556,216	$37,632,141	55,200,011	$1,796,760,358.05	$232,527,002
NHA	12/31/2003	$1.03	$39,958,567	$5,552,325	7,000,111	$7,210,114.33	$45,656,578
High		$32.55	$195,556,216	$37,632,141	100,555,232	$2,287,631,528	$232,527,002
Low		$1.03	$39,958,567	$5,552,325	7,000,111	$7,210,114	$32,577,789
Average		$14.74	$92,198,885	$15,755,014	38,318,646	$868,841,110	$103,841,865

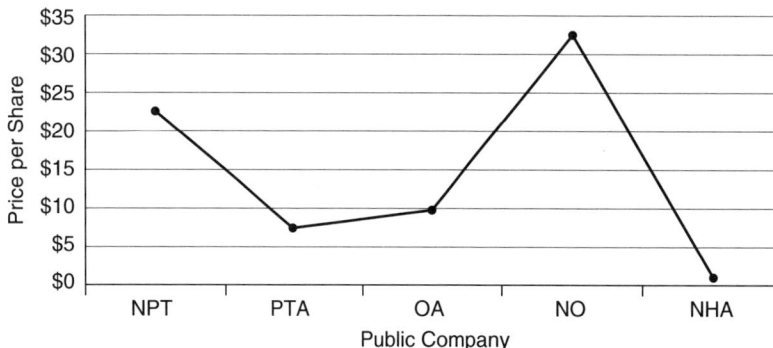

value on the company. When valuing the control interest of a stock that is very nonmarketable, this method is usually the most preferable. However, data from various transactions may be more difficult to find and discern due to the nonpublic nature of the transactions. There are numerous firms that gather this type of data that would prove to be useful (see Appendix B). This form of market valuation is often referred to as the *similar transaction methodology* (or the *guideline merged and acquired company method*).

Both of these methodologies will be discussed in more detail in the following sections.

Normalization and Adjustments to Data

Once the guideline company(s) has been determined, both quantitative financial information and qualitative information on the companies must be compared. This will usually require certain adjustments to the information so that the guideline companies more resemble the subject company, though it is often the case that adjustments will be made to the subject company in order to better resemble the guideline companies (especially if the guideline companies are similar to one another and the subject company is the "outlier"). This process is called *normalizing the data*.

By choosing similar guideline companies, hopefully companies that have many of the same attributes can be found and used in the comparison. This is referred to as normalizing. When normalizing, the subject and the guideline company(s) are made as equal as possible. This method, in fact, is used in some form in all methods of determining value.

In the case of medical practices, whether operated as a sole proprietorship or other legal entities, they often include expenses not typically found nor required within the entities. These are referred to as *discretionary* or *nonoperating expenses*.

For example, consider the case in which the providers in a practice have historically been paid considerably more (or less) than the average for their specialty. This would, therein, make it difficult to compare their expenses to those of the guideline company. While this is not considered illegal or unethical, it is something that must be addressed. To make a legitimate comparison, the appraiser must have the same underlying assumptions at both companies.

Table 3-1 illustrates practice expenses and those adjustments that will ultimately result in a restated or normalized figure. In this example, the appraiser has increased/reduced certain expenses, particularly those deemed above the normal expenses for this particular practice, including physician compensation, benefits, automobiles, donations, travel, etc.

Furthermore, the appraiser must restate any *nonrecurring expenses*. These are expenses that are not regular deductions, such as rent, utilities, or employee compensation, but rather expenditures related to onetime occurrences. For example, in a medical practice, these may be associated with such items as a temporary increase in legal and consulting fees or a special charge due to expanding services. While this may be a legitimate expense, it is not something that is expected

TABLE 3-1

Normalization Process

Expenses	FY 2003	Adjustments*	Normalized Expenses
Personnel expenses			
Physician benefits[†]	$155,656	$13,982	$141,674
Physician compensation[‡]	$695,125	($13,243)	$708,368
Staff benefits	$75,025	$0	$0
Staff salary	$315,151	$0	$0
Total personnel expenses	*$1,240,957*	*$739*	*$850,042*
G&A expenses			
Advertising and promotion	$35,252	$0	$35,252
Amortization	$14,500	$0	$14,500
Automotive[§]	$15,325	$15,325	$0
CME (4)	$4,985	$4,985	$0
Depreciation	$75,895	$0	$75,895
Dues and subscriptions	$4,567	$4,567	$0
Insurance	$55,011	$0	$55,011
Interest expense	$75,898	$0	$75,898
Laundry	$1,255	$0	$1,255
Leased equipment	$4,035	$0	$4,035
Outside services	$4,585	$0	$4,585
Payroll expense	$8,211	$0	$8,211
Professional fees[¶]	$85,426	$50,426	$35,000
Professional liability	$155,252	$0	$155,252
Rental expense	$135,000	$0	$135,000
Supplies: computer	$5,688	$0	$5,688
Supplies: laboratory	$80,122	$0	$80,122
Supplies: medical	$135,002	$0	$135,002
Supplies: office	$20,133	$0	$20,133
Travel and entertainment[‖]	$7,022	$7,022	$0
Utilities	$52,023	$0	$52,023
Total G&A expenses	*$975,187*	*$82,325*	*$892,862*
Total Expenses	$2,216,144	$83,064	$1,742,904

*Negative represents addition of expenses

[†]Adjusted to 20% of physician compensation

[‡]Adjusted to market salary

[§]Automotive not related to the practice

[¶]Nonrecurring consulting fees

[‖]Discretionary expenses

to occur on a regular basis. *(Appraiser beware: Some organizations will classify some expenses as nonrecurring, such as a malpractice settlement or the lawyer fees pertaining to a malpractice case, which, in most instances, is fine. However, if it is noted that the practice, for example, has had charges pertaining to malpractice settlements and lawyer fees consistently throughout the review period, and beyond, it may not be correct to just assume that these are nonrecurring.)*

Depending on the situation (particularly if it is a sole proprietorship or a smaller group), the physician's compensation should be restated or not considered at all. Often, provider compensation will be considered as a *below the line* item from normal operating expenses.

Choose and Apply the Multiple

Once guideline companies have been chosen and the information is adjusted and normalized to make it similar, the information from the guideline companies must be used to calculate the value of the subject company. As previously stated, it is helpful to use public companies because of the great amount of information that is available; however, the appraiser must delve deeper into the guideline company's operations than just determining its stock price. "In fact, due to differences between companies, just a stock price for the guideline company will often prove useless. This is why we must calculate various multiples of the stock prices of the guideline companies in relation to such things as their earnings, cash flow, book value, etc."[2]

Some of the more common multiples include the following:

- Stock price/net (pretax) earnings
- Invested capital/EBIT
- Stock price/cash flow
- Invested capital/EBITDA
- Stock price/sales
- Invested capital/sales

While some of those multiples may be unfamiliar, some of them, such as price to earnings (P/E) and invested capital to earnings before interest, taxes, depreciation, and amortization (IC/EBITDA), may be more familiar. And, while all of them serve a very distinct purpose, not all of them will be applicable to the guideline company or subject company. This is a situation in which the appraiser must use good judgment to determine the most appropriate multiples to apply to the subject company. "The appraiser must utilize both quantitative and qualitative analysis to choose the ratio (multiple) best suited to the subject company."[3]

Bear in mind that the guideline companies may differ from the subject companies; therefore, certain adjustments to the ratios may need to be made before they can be adequately applied. "The appraiser must identify the guideline companies with the most similar growth, trends, and financial profile, and if these profiles do not adequately measure up to the subject company's 'risk' profile then the appraiser must subjectively adjust for these differences."[4] This is considered quantitative analysis.

The guideline companies will likely also differ in ways that cannot be determined by any figures, though certainly they may affect the inherent risk of the guideline company. Adjustments must be made to account for these qualitative differences. The list of qualitative differences may include a number of variables, some of the more common include:

- Size
- Geographic location
- Managed care population/reliance
- Services offered
- Provider and management depth, etc

Another ratio that is commonly used when comparing subject and guideline companies is called the *invested capital (IC) method*. "This method can be particularly good to use when completing a control valuation or the minority interest valuation. Invested capital, or the weighted average cost of capital (WACC), is the market value of the guideline company's equity plus the market value of the interest paying debt, which takes the place of the 'price' in the above multiples. Add the interest paid on the debt to the denominator in the above multiples, adjust for qualitative and quantitative differences, compute the fair market value estimate and deduct the fair market value of the subject's debt to reach a value of the equity."[5]

Figure 3-2 illustrates examples of various multiples that may be derived using the IC method of determining the multiple from 3 different corporations.

Using multiples based on IC allows a comparison without adjusting for differing degrees of financial leverage, which can hinder using companies that are debt-laden.

Similar Transaction Method

Another excellent source of data is from previous transactions that have taken place. Consider the example in Figure 3-3. In order to place an appropriate multiple on the subject company, similar recent transactions have to be used. These can often be a good resource when data is hard to find, although this data can also be difficult to accumulate if the acquiring company is not a publicly held entity. Also, one must consider a number of other issues, such as the date of the transaction and the size of the acquired company. These can all play a role in the application of the multiple to the subject company.

The *similar transaction method*, or *acquisition method*, does carry with it a number of advantages and disadvantages, although it is in the appraiser's judgment to determine if one outweighs the other. Some of the advantages include the following[6]:

- Can provide the best indication of the prices at which entire entities/practices change hands
- Objective source of data
- Informed buyers and sellers

Some of the disadvantages include the following:

- Hard to find similar companies that have been acquired
- Hard to find data on the acquisitions
- Hard to interpret the data and what exactly is being bought and sold
- May involve specific buyers that will pay a premium for special or unique considerations

FIGURE **3-2**

Summary of Public Company Market Multiples

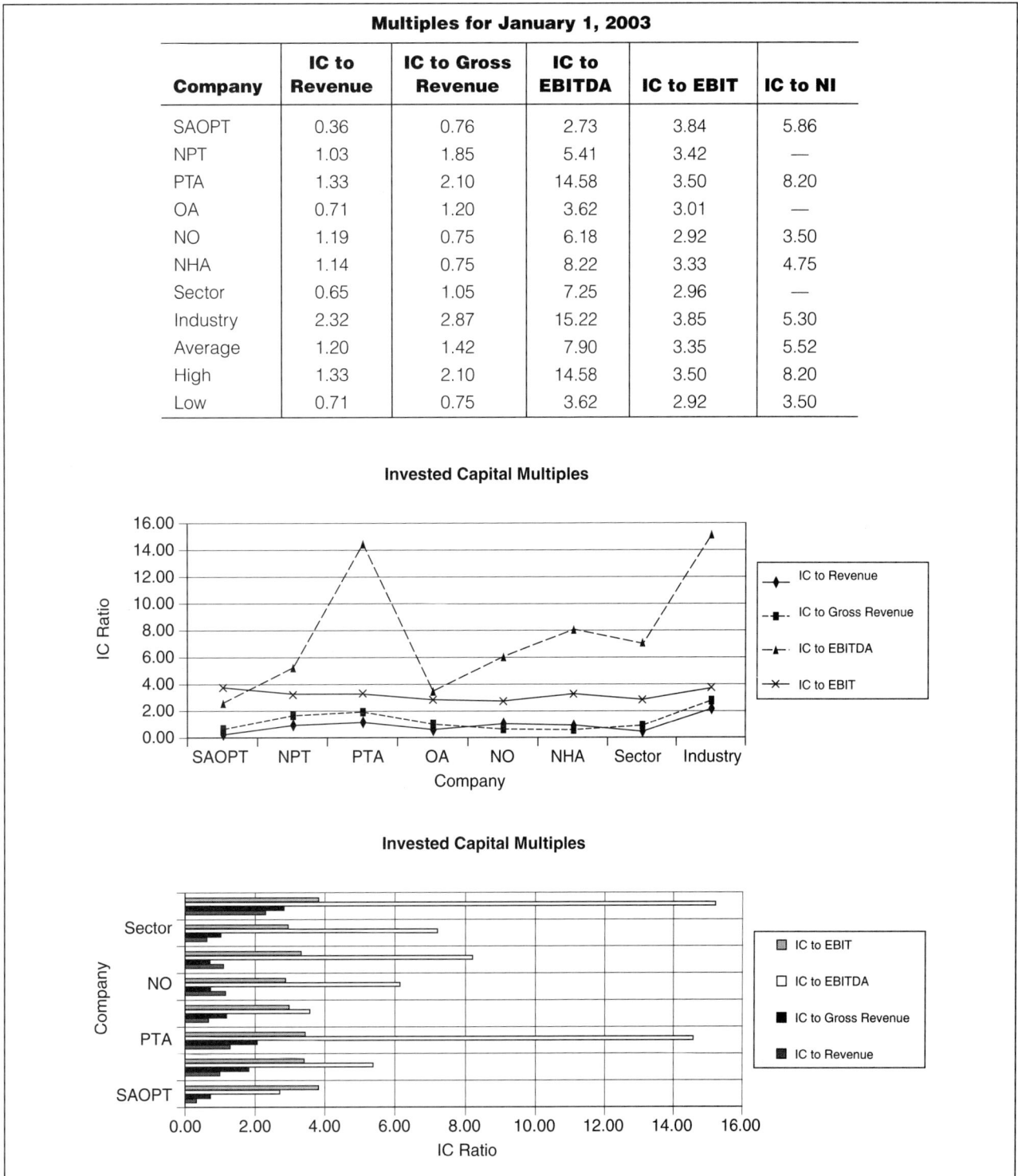

Multiples for January 1, 2003

Company	IC to Revenue	IC to Gross Revenue	IC to EBITDA	IC to EBIT	IC to NI
SAOPT	0.36	0.76	2.73	3.84	5.86
NPT	1.03	1.85	5.41	3.42	—
PTA	1.33	2.10	14.58	3.50	8.20
OA	0.71	1.20	3.62	3.01	—
NO	1.19	0.75	6.18	2.92	3.50
NHA	1.14	0.75	8.22	3.33	4.75
Sector	0.65	1.05	7.25	2.96	—
Industry	2.32	2.87	15.22	3.85	5.30
Average	1.20	1.42	7.90	3.35	5.52
High	1.33	2.10	14.58	3.50	8.20
Low	0.71	0.75	3.62	2.92	3.50

Invested Capital Multiples

Invested Capital Multiples

Discounts and Premiums Applied to Market Multiples

These multiples from both methods (ie, similar transaction method and market multiple method) provide us with excellent information on which to base the value of the subject company, though, one must

F I G U R E 3-3

Similar Transaction Method (Acquisition Data)

Target	Date	Revenue	Net Income	Total Assets	Invested Capital	Transaction Price	Price to Revenue	Price to Income	Price to Assets	Price to Invested Capital
PTSC	07/01/96	$9,585,235	$53,252	$6,252,535	$5,663,210	$22,523,852	2.3498487	422.9672501	3.602355205	3.977223518
SP	04/01/01	$95,251,325	$3,258,958	$29,024,361	$28,974,069	$89,593,262	0.94059859	27.49138283	3.086829784	3.09218777
OAK	06/01/01	$5,253,250	$111,235	$334,558	$279,090	$7,532,892	1.433948889	67.72051962	22.51595239	26.99090616
HS	05/01/02	$33,589,257	$989,585	$19,992,536	$19,892,284	$35,896,552	1.068691457	36.27434935	1.79549768	1.804546527
NOC	09/01/02	$25,869,252	$979,798	$55,252	$54,227	$32,589,027	1.259759153	33.26096502	589.8252914	600.9741826
RAN	01/01/03	$2,358,952	($225,896)	$746,212	$672,691	$852,325	0.361315109	-3.773085845	1.142202216	1.267037912
High		$95,251,325	$3,258,958	$29,024,361	$28,974,069	$89,593,262	2.35	422.97	589.83	600.97
Low		$2,358,952	($225,896)	$55,252	$54,227	$852,325	0.36	(3.77)	1.14	1.27
Average		$28,651,212	$861,155	$9,400,909	$9,255,929	$31,497,985	1.24	97.32	103.66	106.35
SAOPT		$2,360,975	$144,831	$889,063	$848,059	$0				

Price to Revenue Multiple to Transaction Date

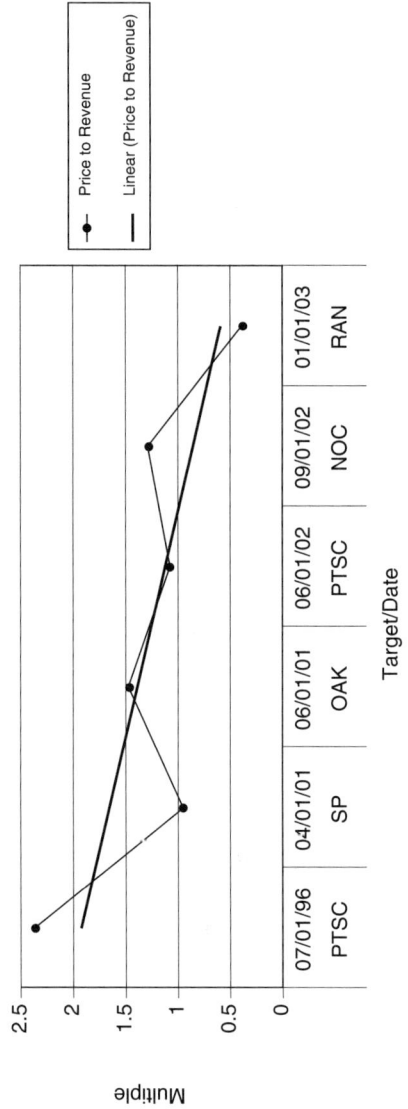

Legend: Price to Revenue; Linear (Price to Revenue)

Y-axis: Multiple (0, 0.5, 1, 1.5, 2, 2.5)

X-axis: Target/Date — 07/01/96 PTSC, 04/01/01 SP, 06/01/01 OAK, 06/01/02 PTSC, 09/01/02 NOC, 01/01/03 RAN

remember that the guideline companies are not comparable but similar. Also, certain extraneous factors may cause the guideline companies to differ from the subject company, such as an economic recession. In such cases, a discount or premium must be added to the multiple of the guideline company so that it may better resemble the subject company.

This is yet another example in which the appraiser's judgment and experience is called into action because placing a discount or premium on a subject company's multiple is strictly subjective.

For instance, consider the appraisal of a majority interest of a large, privately held multiple specialty medical practice (eg, a privately held physician practice management company). All of the guideline companies that have been used to calculate the market multiples may have been based on the minority interest of large publicly held practices.

It is likely that the controlling interest of an entity is worth more than a minority interest because with control comes the ability to make operations-altering decisions. A minority interest usually does not have such control. Furthermore, if minority interests are used to place multiples on a control valuation, it is likely that a premium will be placed on the guideline company's multiple to reflect the controlling interest.

Conversely, while a controlling interest may call for a premium on a guideline company's multiple, the fact that the company is closely held may require a discount to be applied. Although a controlling interest may mean that a single person may significantly determine the plight of the company, this significantly affects that person's ability to buy and sell all or portions of the company or their marketability. However, a publicly owned company is easy to exchange and is one of the most liquid financial holdings.

Does this mean that the premium for controlling interest will cancel out the discount of lack of marketability? This is when the value of a knowledgeable appraiser can provide invaluable skill and advice. In all likelihood, the discount for lack of marketability will outweigh the control interest premium, though, this is a hypothetical situation and actualities are impossible to determine.

There are no tables in which to find answers to the aforementioned situation. Certainly, the appraiser can examine past appraisals that are available to the public to help understand how previous discounts and premiums were applied and how they affected that appraiser's decisions. In addition, there are volumes of studies that have been completed that try to address this matter. Though, this process is primarily one that is subjective and will rely heavily on the assumptions and reasoning behind such applications and the application of these studies.

Calculate the Value

When the adjustments have been made and the appropriate multiples have been chosen, these must be applied to the company so that the value can be determined. This is the final step in calculating the value of the subject company.

Once the appropriate multiple is calculated based on the market multiple or similar transaction methods from the best-suited guideline company (more than one company can be averaged if one specific company does not offer the best representation), this multiple should be applied to the subject company. For example, in Figure 3-2, the average IC/Revenue multiple for the guideline companies is 1.2. Multiply this ratio of IC/Revenues by the subject company's revenues of $2,360,975 and a total value of $2,833,170 is calculated. However, because IC was used, the appropriate level of interest-bearing debt for the subject company must be subtracted in order to determine the equity value (ie, approximately $427,730; see balance sheet example in Appendix A). Before any discounts or premiums, this would calculate a volume of $2,405,440 based on the market multiple method.

If price to revenues was used under the similar transaction method in Figure 3-2, and the average for the guideline companies was 1.24. This would then be multiplied by the subject company's revenues of $2,360,975 to equal $2,927,609 (again before the application of any discounts or premiums). However, because the IC was not used and this is only the value of the company's equity, debt does not have to be subtracted.

Based on this analysis, one can see that the values associated with the different ratios (multiples) will vary, though both cases are before the application of any discounts or premiums. Depending on the value being sought and the market figures that are used, these may considerably affect the value.

The market valuation and the application of various multiples have been considerably simplified for demonstration purposes. It is assumed that any quantitative and qualitative adjustments have already been made before any calculation of value commences. Also, the most viable multiples may not be an average. Again, this process has been somewhat oversimplified for demonstration purposes.

Source of Market Data

In order to perform a viable market analysis of a company, necessary data must be available to perform the analysis. In fact, an appraiser will likely have more trouble sorting through all of the data that has been gathered rather than finding enough information.

As noted, public companies provide a wealth of information that can be used as market data. And, while each of the companies differs in many ways, the appraiser should know how to apply the appropriate premiums and discounts to make the information more applicable. We have provided numerous resources in Appendix B from which an appraiser of a business could obtain a large amount of information.

Nonapplicability of the Market Approach

Something that has not been addressed to this point that is applicable to valuing entities, such as a medical practice, is the lack of data for small practices. This whole section has stressed the importance of finding guideline companies to use as similar companies in which to base market multiples. And, the majority of these companies are larger, publicly traded entities that may not be applicable to a smaller practice.

Data in which to base market multiples used to value extremely small companies may be difficult to obtain, though, not impossible. Plus, much of the data will be for much larger entities; entities so large that considerable discounts to the market multiples would not be enough to make them applicable. However, some analysts that want to include the market approach within their valuation for smaller, harder-to-find-information-on entities will revert to the Goodwill Registry. This is a registry of various multiples for smaller entities that can be applied to the subject company. Often these are referred to as "rules of thumb."

In the past, the Goodwill Registry has been considered an appropriate source of data, and at one time valuations of medical practices were completed based solely on those multiples derived from the Goodwill Registry. However, this has become less accepted in the value of medical practices and other entities, for that matter.

Furthermore, there is a wide consensus in the valuation community against the use of rules of thumbs, as noted, ". . . It is essential to remember that industry formulas or rules of thumb are commonly not market derived representations of actual transactions. Since most industry formulas or rules of thumb are derived from textbooks, trade publications, verbal representations or other similar sources of information, they are poor substitutes for the Direct Market Comparison Approach."[7]

Now that it has been noted that Goodwill Registry is not the best method of determining market multiples and other data can be difficult, if not impossible, to find, what does an appraiser do? If this is the case, an analyst may make the decision that the market approach does not apply in this situation. Instead, the analyst may weight the other 2 methods (asset-based approach or income approach) more heavily.

In fact, this is not such an irregular occurrence, and in order to appropriately address this issue, the exclusion of one of the standards of value is permitted under the Uniform Standards of Professional Appraisal Practice (USPAP), Standards Rule 9-4(a),[8] to wit,

> An appraiser must develop value opinion(s) and conclusions(s) by use of one or more approaches that apply to the specific appraisal assignment;
>
> **Comment**: This rule requires the appraiser to use all relevant approaches for which sufficient reliable data are available. However, it does not mean that the appraiser must use all approaches in order to comply with the rule if certain approaches are not applicable.

Just because an appraiser has been tasked to value a small entity in which it may be difficult to find similar market data, does not mean the appraiser should discard the market approach before beginning on the project. The proper due diligence should be made to determine if this method is applicable, and if it is not, the analyst should explain in detail the motives and reasoning for not using the market approach.

Market Approach Conclusion

As one can see, the market approach most often requires an investment of a large amount of research and time to accurately calculate the applied multiples to the subject company. This method requires a great deal of subjectivity when determining how to apply the various multiples that are calculated. And, while it may not be the best for smaller, closely held medical practices (eg, a solo practitioner), it is an indispensable method that should certainly be considered in valuations of all sizes.

ASSET-BASED APPROACH

The asset-based approach uses a number of different methods to value both tangible and intangible assets on a going-concern basis.

This value is often utilized to value an entity that is going out of business or discontinuing operations; however, it can also be used as a supporting valuation of a going-concern. Some experts share the idea that the asset-based approach is not best suited for service companies (eg, a medical practice) or to value the intangible assets of a company. However, in cases where the market approach is not applicable and the income approach (discussed later) calculates a negative value, this may be the only method in which any value can be applied to an entity. In this case it is perfectly acceptable.

Tangible Asset Value

In Chapter 1, tangible assets were defined and several examples were presented. Tangible assets consist of physician items, such as equipment, furniture, supplies, fixtures, cash, accounts receivable, inventory, etc. For purposes of this initial review, tangible assets are limited only to those items, such as equipment, furniture, and the like.

For accounting purposes, most of these tangible assets have a depreciable value that is reduced over a specific period of time—usually over a period of years—depending on the method of depreciation used. However, tangible assets are generally worth more than their depreciable value, or their book value (ie, original cost minus accumulated depreciation). For example, if a medical practice purchases an exam table, and depreciates that exam table over a period of 5 years, at the end of that 5-year period that exam table will be completely depreciated and it will have no book value. Nevertheless, this does not mean that the practice would just give this exam table away for free because it has no book value. This exemplifies why book value may not be the best method of valuing tangible assets. In fact, the following are a number of ways in which to value tangible assets aside from book value[9]:

- **Reproduction cost new**:   The cost of reproducing a new replica of an item on the basis of current prices with the same or closely similar materials
- **Replacement cost new**:   The current cost of a similar new item having the nearest equivalent utility as the item being appraised

■ **Depreciated replacement cost new**: Replacement cost new less depreciation

■ **Fair market value in continued use (in-place value)**: The fair market value of an item based on its original purchase price and the continued utilization of the item in conjunction with all other installed items

■ **Liquidation value**: Amount expected by the immediate sale of the assets, includes:

— **Orderly liquidation**

— **Forced liquidation**

For purposes of valuing a medical practice, the appraiser will most often be concerned with only the in-place value and the liquidation value.

In-place Value

The *in-place value* method assumes that the equipment has greater value to the purchaser of the equipment because it is in-place and plays an integral role in the generation of revenue.

The in-place value is calculated by taking a number of issues into consideration, such as the ability to purchase all of the equipment at one time rather than having to go find each item individually, the type of equipment, the usability of the equipment in its current position, and, most importantly, the condition of the equipment. The appraiser applies these qualitative standards and formulates an *in-place percentage*. As noted throughout the valuation process, the appraiser applies a great deal of subjectivity.

While there are some standards as to the percentage that is applied, based primarily on its condition and usability (see Table 3-2), there are no finite determinations as to the calculation of these percentages.

One reason why these are purely suggestions rather than standards is that these percentages truly vary from item to item based on a wide range of issues. For instance, consider a computer system that was purchased 18 months ago and is in excellent condition. Judging by Table 3-2, an in-place percentage of 70% to 80% should theoretically be applied. Technology—such as computers, printers, and faxes—typically retains less value than other equipment because of its obsolescence rate. For this reason, the subjectivity that must be applied to calculate this percentage becomes apparent.

T A B L E 3-2

In-place Value Percentages

Condition	In-place Percentage
Brand new	85-100
Excellent	70-85
Good	60-70
Fair	45-60
Poor	15-45
Scrap	0-15

Once the in-place percentage that will be applied to the item has been determined, the item's value must be calculated. To do this, the in-place percentage is multiplied by the item's original cost. While this may seem fairly straightforward, it may not be so easy to determine the asset's original value. If the entity, or practice in this case, has kept good records over the years, then it should have the original cost of the items, though, this is frequently not the case. In fact, most medical practices, especially smaller ones, typically keep poor records of these items. If the entity cannot provide these documents, the appraiser must determine the approximate cost of the items.

This can be difficult for the appraiser because of the extent to which items differ. Medical equipment is generally easier because it is highly identifiable (eg, a Ritter 104 exam table, a GE x-ray machine). Office equipment, on the other hand, can be more difficult to determine. For example, without a thorough inspection—likely by someone familiar with furniture construction—it would be difficult to determine if a physician's executive desk set is custom-made mahogany or the manufactured set made to look like the custom-made set. Again, the appraiser has to use good judgment and determine what is a correct price.

An appraiser should take into consideration the age of the item and the fact that an item bought 30 years ago would almost certainly have cost less than an item bought within the last few years. Though, an appraiser could apply the same cost to the same items, say for example exam tables, but build this discount in price into the in-place percentage. Regardless of the method used by the appraiser, it is essential that the appraiser clearly and consistently states all assumptions within the report.

When valuing the assets of a smaller entity, the appraiser can make a detailed list of the assets and value each one individually (as is done in Table 3-3). However, in medium to larger entities this would likely be impossible. In this case, the appraiser may have to combine the different items per the tangible asset inventory from the entity's federal tax returns (an excellent place to get information such as number of and original purchase price of the entity's assets) and organize them by category, as shown in Table 3-4.

The in-place method of valuing tangible assets is one of the most accepted methodologies in valuing the assets in a going concern. It takes into consideration the asset's value over and above that typically referred to as book value and focuses many of those aspects of an asset that book value does not consider.

Liquidation Value

If in-place value is the valuing of an entity's assets as a going concern and valuing them for future use in that going concern, then liquidation value can be seen as just the opposite. *Liquidation value* is the valuing of an entity's assets that will close or not continue as a going concern.

Typically, when one hears the term *liquidation*, a hardship is implied. This, however, is not always the case. For example, an entity that chooses to discontinue business for no specific reason ceases operations as an ongoing entity. Before the entity can be fully dissolved,

TABLE 3-3

Tangible Asset Inventory Valuation for a Small Entity

Practice	Quantity	Unit Value	Total Value	In-Place Percentage	In-Place Value
Front office					
Secretary chair	3	$100	$300	50%	$150
Typewriter, Panasonic	1	$150	$150	20%	$30
Back office					
Desk, wood	1	$250	$250	55%	$138
Bookcase	1	$200	$200	55%	$110
Desk, Formica	1	$250	$250	55%	$138
Break room					
Bookcase	1	$95	$95	55%	$52
Waiting room					
Waiting chair	20	$100	$2,000	45%	$900
Side table	5	$50	$250	45%	$113
Nurses station					
Temp-Plus II	2	$210	$420	60%	$252
Secretary chair	2	$100	$200	50%	$100
Filing cabinet, lateral, 3-drawer	2	$645	$1,290	50%	$645
Exam room 12					
Exam table, flat, wood	1	$300	$300	55%	$165
Rolling stool	1	$90	$90	55%	$50
Step	1	$25	$25	55%	$14
Otoscope/ophthalmoscope, Welch Allyn	1	$500	$500	55%	$275
Total			**$6,320**		**$3,310**

TABLE 3-4

Tangible Asset Inventory Valuation for a Medium to Large Entity

	Total Items	Total Cost	In-Place Percentage	In-Place Value
Medical equipment	2,653	$560,230	60%	$336,138
Furniture	10,552	$3,342,502	50%	$1,671,251
Office equipment (not including computers)	335	$255,022	45%	$114,760
Total		**$4,157,754**		**$2,122,149**

it must dispose of all of its tangible (as well as intangible) assets. In this case, an appraiser would assign the assets an *orderly liquidation value*. "That is the proceeds that one could expect from the sale of the assets held under normal conditions given a reasonable period of time in which to find a purchaser and sell the assets 'as is, where is,' with the purchaser assuming the cost of all removal and other related costs."[10]

The other type of liquidation, *forced liquidation*, occurs when a company must liquidate assets for the purpose of quickly offloading assets (whether the majority or a portion of the assets) for one reason or another. Usually, forced liquidation occurs when there is no time to find a purchaser. This situation could arise for a number of reasons. For example, a company may be forced to liquidate some of its assets to cover a short-term debt that has come due or to close out a facility as dictated by a landlord. This is often referred to as a *fire sale*.

The difference between the 2 types of liquidations is essentially the time involved. In one instance, an entity has unlimited time to find a willing buyer; in the other, they do not.

Both the forced liquidation and the orderly liquidation can be calculated in the same manner as in-place value through the application of an in-place percentage to the original cost. However, with liquidations, some type of discount is applied to the in-place percentage. Typically, the orderly liquidation method will have a minimal discount applied to it, likely something around 15% to 20%. This takes into account that the purchaser is buying "as is, where is," and that they will incur more costs due to moving and storage fees (that would not be incurred if the assets were going to be used in the same place and for the same reason).

Forced liquidation on the other hand will usually command much more of a discount to the in-place percentage. In the situation of a fire sale, or forced liquidation, a discount of 50% to 65%, depending upon the situation and the item, will be incurred.

For example, the previous exhibits (Tables 3-3 and 3-4), when converted to an orderly liquidation and a fire sale (Tables 3-5 and 3-6, respectively), illustrate the effect of tangible assets on value.

Other Tangible Assets

Both the in-place valuation methodology and the liquidation methodology are used to value an entity's actual equipment, which most people refer to as *tangible assets*. However, tangible assets include not just those items that can be touched and felt (eg, equipment, furniture). Items such as cash, accounts receivable, notes receivable, etc, are also considered tangible assets. While these items are different from equipment and furniture, they certainly do represent tangible assets attributable to the entity and therein potentially valuable to the entity.

The best place to determine an entity's assets is from the balance sheet. Most medical practices—especially the smaller ones—pay little, if any, attention to the balance sheet (as opposed to a larger entity where the balance sheet is a key financial management tool). This is because most medical practices complete their accounting on the cash basis (or a modified cash basis), thus making the balance sheet somewhat useless. In fact, because of this, calculating a smaller practice's tangible asset value is often not completed (though it certainly does have applicability in regards to medium and larger organizations).

The first step in determining a practice's asset value is calculating its assets. While this appears to be as easy as adding all of the assets from the balance sheet to determine the value, it is not quite that simple. Actually, an appraiser must complete a considerable amount of analysis in order to determine the correct number associated with each of the asset categories. To do this, the appraiser must determine the adjusted book value of each of the asset categories.

TABLE 3-5

Orderly and Forced Liquidation Valuation for a Small Entity

Practice	Quantity	Unit Value	Total Value	Orderly Liquidation Percentage	Orderly Liquidation Value	Forced Liquidation Percentage	Forced Liquidation Value
Front office							
Secretary chair	3	$100	$300	43%	$128	17.50%	$53
Typewriter, Panasonic	1	$150	$150	17%	$26	7.00%	$11
Back office							
Desk, wood	1	$250	$250	47%	$117	19.25%	$48
Bookcase	1	$200	$200	47%	$94	19.25%	$39
Desk, Formica	1	$250	$250	47%	$117	19.25%	$48
Break room							
Bookcase	1	$95	$95	47%	$44	19.25%	$18
Waiting room							
Waiting chair	20	$100	$2,000	38%	$765	15.75%	$315
Side table	5	$50	$250	38%	$96	15.75%	$39
Nurses station							
Temp-Plus II	2	$210	$420	51%	$214	21.00%	$88
Secretary chair	2	$100	$200	43%	$85	17.50%	$35
Filing cabinet, lateral, 3-drawer	2	$645	$1,290	43%	$548	17.50%	$226
Exam room 12							
Exam table, flat, wood	1	$300	$300	47%	$140	19.25%	$58
Rolling stool	1	$90	$90	47%	$42	19.25%	$17
Step	1	$25	$25	47%	$12	19.25%	$5
Otoscope/ophthalmoscope, Welch Allyn	1	$500	$500	47%	$234	19.25%	$96
Total			**$6,320**		**$2,661**		**$1,096**

TABLE 3-6

Orderly and Forced Liquidation Valuation for a Large Entity

	Total Items	Total Cost	Orderly Liquidation In-Place Percentage	Orderly Liquidation Price	Forced Liquidation Percentage	Forced Liquidation Price
Medical equipment	2,653	$560,230	60.00%	$285,717	21.00%	$117,648
Furniture	10,552	$3,342,502	50.00%	$1,420,563	17.50%	$584,938
Office equipment (not including computers)	335	$255,022	45.00%	$97,546	15.75%	$40,166
Total		**$4,157,754**		**$1,803,827**		**$742,752**

The key to determining adjusted book value is to make sure that the appraiser has adjusted all of the assets to fair market value, which must include the intangibles if under consideration for value. When considering whether to value intangibles, one must determine whether (1) the entity does or does not have intangible value and (2) the purchaser is interested in intangible assets or just the tangible assets.

In order to determine fair market value for the tangible assets, the appraiser must adjust the assets currently on the balance sheet. In some cases this may not be applicable; for instance, cash on a balance sheet would require no adjustment because $1,000 cash on hand in the bank for the current owner will be worth $1,000 cash on hand in the bank for the purchaser. However, the item that will almost always need to be restated is that of accounts receivable (A/R). This is because A/R on an entity's book, or A/R's book value, is almost always not that which will actually be collected. In fact, valuing A/R could entail a whole chapter of this book, if not a whole book itself. For purposes of this analysis, a company's A/R book value will be more than that which is actually collectable (often referred to as *fair collectable value*).

Another reason to determine a practice's adjusted book value is to ensure that not only the fair market value of the assets have been taken into account but also its liabilities. In valuing a company's assets, outstanding liabilities must be determined and the net of those liabilities must be determined against the company's assets. If the assets are less than the liabilities, the practice exhibits no net tangible asset value.

Two of the major adjustments to assets are exhibited in Table 3-7 in the adjusted balance sheet.

Because this methodology can often not pertain to a smaller entity, the determining of an entity's asset value will often be based on one of the previously stated methods of in-place or liquidation value, or via one of the following methodologies. In fact, most appraisers of smaller practices will make the assumption that the transfer of ownership will include only the tangible items, such as furniture and equipment, and the other items, such as cash and accounts receivable, and the resulting liabilities will not be considered as part of the transfer. This simplifies the process, but such steps must be implicitly stated in the valuation. For example, if a practice's intangible value is calculated at $100,000 and it does not include debt and the practice has $90,000 in debt, then the fair value of the debt will have to be netted against the equity value or it must be assumed that the purchaser will not be *assuming* this level of debt.

Intangible Asset Values

It has been noted that in determining the fair market value, a company's tangible and intangible assets must be considered. Often, larger corporations will consider the intangible asset value on the balance sheets as goodwill, and thus, when determining the net asset value, this goodwill must be applied. However, in smaller practices, the appropriate method of determining the intangible value is via a separate calculation, then adding that to the tangible asset value that has been calculated. The best methods for determining the intangible asset value of an entity are the excess earnings methodology (which includes the capitalization of earnings methodology) and the weighted earnings methodology.

In determining the figures to use for these methodologies, because they are based on historical figures, the appraiser will use an average

TABLE 3-7

Balance Sheet Adjustments

	FY 2003 Balance Sheet	Adjustments	FY 2003 Balance Sheet Adjusted
Assets			
Current assets			
Cash (money market account)	$12,502	$0	$12,502
Accounts receivable*	$225,898	($75,898)	$150,000
Total current assets	*$238,400*	*($75,898)*	*$162,502*
Long-term assets			
Property, plant, & equipment†	$753,252	($75,325)	$677,927
Accumulated depreciation	$102,589	$0	$0
Total long-term assets	*$650,663*	*($75,325)*	*$677,927*
Total Assets	**$889,063**		**$840,429**
Liabilities			
Current liabilities			
Accounts payable	$5,252	$0	$5,252
Short-term debt	$15,250	$0	$15,250
Total current liabilities	*$20,502*	*$0*	*$20,502*
Long-term liabilities			
Long-term debt			
Eastern Bank loan	$372,609	$0	$372,609
Central Bank line of credit	$55,121	$0	$55,121
Total long-term liabilities	*$427,730*	*$0*	*$427,730*
Total liabilities	**$448,232**	**$0**	**$448,232**
Equity	**$420,329**	**$0**	**$420,329**
Total Liabilities and Equity	**$889,063**	**$0**	**$889,063**

*Discounted to fair collectible value.

†Discount based on in-place value of furniture and equipment.

of the entity's most recent operating figures (eg, normalized expenses, revenues), usually between the last 3 to 5 years.

Excess Earnings Method

The excess earnings method, or formula method, is derived from IRS Revenue Ruling 68-609. This method attempts to value the intangible assets by considering appropriate returns on both tangible and intangible assets. Under most circumstances, normalized historical operating results would be utilized; however, if it is deemed appropriate by the analyst, recent operating results can be substituted.

This methodology is fairly straightforward, although, as has been the case in the past, the appraiser must make certain projections that are very subjective. In this case, the appraiser must determine the correct rate of return and capitalization rate. Ultimately, the best way to support all subjective figures is still through thorough documentation of the underlying assumptions.

The following describes some simple procedures used to calculate the value in Figure 3-4:

Step 1: The appraiser must determine the market value of tangible assets and the normalized level of income.

   a. The methods used to determine an entity's tangible asset value have been discussed previously in this chapter. The value determined by the appraiser by the appropriate standard of value will be applied here.

   b. The appraiser must determine the appropriate level of earnings. The appraiser must determine whether to use normalized or actual earnings. Still, the appraiser must determine the appropriate time frame that is being considered. The basic premise behind this model is that it relies on historic information.

Step 2: This step is done to determine the level of excess earnings. This is done in the following parts:

   a. First, the appraiser must determine an appropriate rate of return on the tangible assets (see Step 1.a). This will usually be similar to the entity's stated cost of capital, or

FIGURE 3-4

Capitalization of Excess Earnings (Formula) Method

Market value of assets*	$840,429
Adjusted net income (loss) 2003†	$313,723
1. Net tangible asset value	$840,429
Rate of return	24%

Excess earnings attributable to net tangible assets
$840,429 × 24% = **$201,703**

Excess earnings
$313,723 − $201,703 = **$112,020**

2. Excess earnings	$112,020
Capitalization rate	21.75%

Excess earnings capitalized
$112,020 ÷ 21.75% = **$515,034**

Total value

Net asset value (tangible)	**$ 840,429**
Excess earnings (intangible)	**$ 515,034**
	$1,355,463

*Market value of assets is based on the in-place value of the practice's furniture and equipment and the fair collection value of the practice's accounts receivable (see Table 3-7).

†Net income is based on the normalized profit (see Appendix A).

in the case of smaller companies that may not know their internal cost of capital, it could be estimated by the analyst. This rate of return is then multiplied by the asset total to determine the excess earnings attributable to the company's net tangible assets.

b. Second, the appraiser will subtract this amount from the normalized net income (see Step 1.b), and this will provide the excess earnings for the company.

Step 3: This step determines the actual intangible value attributable to the entity. This is done by capitalizing the excess earnings by an appropriate capitalization rate (discount rate minus long-term growth).

Step 4: The appraiser will add the intangible value (see Step 3) and the tangible value (see Step 2), which will provide the appraiser with the total value of the entity.

While these steps are generally accepted as the traditional formula approach, various other methodologies have been used under this approach. This provides an accurate approach to valuing an entity, but it only considers the company's historical operations, which is helpful but not what one wants when trying to determine the on-going value of a company.

Weighted Earnings Method

The weighted earnings method is used to consider patterns of expenses and revenue. Within this method, each component is adjusted by a factor that reflects its relative importance to the whole by multiplying each component by its assigned weight or degree of significance. The weighted average is derived by adding the product and then dividing the sum of the product by the sum of the weights. See Figure 3-5 for a calculation example.

Asset-based Approach Conclusion

The ways in which to value not only a practice's actual tangible assets but also the practice's intangible assets are numerous. One must bear in mind that when calculating both the tangible and intangible assets via the 2 methodologies, the 2 figures must be combined in order to determine the total value of the entity.

While these methodologies may not suit entities such as a medical practice, they can provide good benchmarks or supporting documentation. Though, in the cases where the entity exhibits no intangible value via the discounted cash flow methodology, the value of the entity's assets may be its only value. For this reason, calculations should virtually always be completed.

INCOME APPROACH

The income approach is the best method that calls for a detailed financial appraisal of an entity (or a portion thereof). The beauty of this approach is that it considers the past operations and financial performance of an entity, then uses these figures in combination with the best estimates of future performance to place a value of the

FIGURE 3-5

Weighted Earnings Method

Year	Collections	Weight	Extension
2000	$1,865,110	1	$1,865,110
2001	$1,963,479	2	3,926,958
2002	$2,075,494	3	6,226,482
2003	$2,360,975	4	9,443,900
Total extension			21,462,450
Divided by weighting			÷ 10
Weighted average collections			2,146,245
Less average practice expense (restated)			(1,869,151)
Weighted net income before provider compensation			277,094
Ratings scale (as follows)			90%
Total value			**$249,384**
Add market value of asset			840,429
Total value			**$1,089,813**

Key to Rating Scale*	Risk Percent
Risk rating (20%)	
■ Continuity of income at risk	
■ Steady income likely	
■ Growing income assured	(18%)
Competitive rating (15%)	
■ Highly competitive and/or unstable market	
■ Normal competitive conditions	
■ Little competition in the market due to high cost of competition entry	(13%)
Specialty rating (20%)	
■ Specialty practice, all physician referral	
■ Specialty practice with high level of primary care	
■ Primary care, no physician referral	(19%)
Business rating (20%)	
■ Recent start-up, not established	
■ Well-established in satisfactory environment	
■ Long record of sound operation with outstanding reputation	(18%)
Business growth (15%)	
■ Business has been declining	
■ Steady growth, slightly higher than inflation rate	
■ Dynamic business growth	(13%)
Desirability rating (10%)	
■ No status, rural area, declining population	
■ Satisfactory environment, population growth, surplus physician/patient	
■ Challenging environment, metropolitan or high growth area, high physician/patient ratio	(9%)
Total	**(90%)**

*This rating represents the risk, stability, and other factors inherent in the medical business.

company. Because the value of anything is the present value of its future cash flows, this method is often referred to as the *discounted cash flow (DCF) methodology*.

As accepted and important as this methodology is, it does, ironically, require more subjectivity from the analyst than any other approach. All of the other methods described up to this point relied on identifiable data that has already occurred (ie, historical), and while there is a level of subjectivity required under these approaches (eg, the in-place percentage under the asset approach, the cost of capital under the capitalization of earnings method), none require the level that is applied under the DCF methodology. The values calculated under the other methodologies consider the company and its past operations, but this will not serve the purposes for valuing an on-going business venture, or more appropriately, the present value of a company's future cash flow.

An analyst must rely on detailed knowledge of the business being valued, the industry in which it competes, as well as the underlying assumptions used in the DCF methodology. This stresses why whenever an analyst is being chosen to complete a valuation of an entity—especially a medical practice—they should exhibit a strong knowledge of the industry that is under consideration.

This section of the chapter provides an overview of the DCF methodology under the income approach and details that which is necessary to calculate the value of an entity under this approach. This chapter, however, will not serve as a "mini MBA" in finance, detailing the minutia and details that form the foundational information that has been developed over the years. The information used to develop this methodology has been spurred by some of the greatest minds to address the subject of finance, economics, accounting, and mathematics and fills volumes and volumes of books.

A lack of focus on this detail does not imply that this information is not significant, rather just the opposite; this methodology requires a detailed understanding of both financial theory and operations. Without such a basis, it would be impossible for anyone to be able to properly utilize the information that will be outlined in this section. Thus, it is assumed that the reader has a general understanding of finance, economics, mathematics, and accounting (amongst others) so that the aspects of this model are not only properly understood, but also properly applied.

If one has a proper understanding of the theory underlying DCF methodology, then he or she can apply the approach to any company. However, the DCF methodology discussed in this book focuses on the valuation of a physician's practice and other health care entities and, as such, some of the techniques used to value a medical practice may not be those best suited for valuing other companies in other industries.

The Return Used to Base Value

Before anything can be valued, the appraiser must first know what is being valued. This does not mean the actual company that is being valued or even the portion of the company (eg, majority interest, minority interest). In this case, the appraiser must know what is being used to determine the value of the company.

Under the asset-based approach, focus is placed on the valuation of the company's assets (ie, the left side of the balance sheet). Under the DCF methodology, focus is placed on the company's debt and equity (ie, the right side of the balance sheet). Thus, in going forward, the appraiser must determine if he or she will value the company's debt and equity or just the company's equity and, depending on the type of investment that will be valued, what return will be used to base the value.

While both the debt and equity may be valued in a company, in focusing on a medical entity, an appraiser will generally want to focus on the valuing of a practice's equity. This is primarily because medical practices and other medical entities in most cases do not carry a large debt load, and if they do, it is likely that there may not be any intangible value. Therefore, the appraiser will most often want to focus on one of the bottom returns or another return associated with equity (ie, excluding debt).

The returns equal the calculated value of the entity. Before a value is calculated, however, knowing how to reach the anticipated stream of income (ie, the return) is key.

Financial operations can be managed in 1 of 2 ways: on the cash basis of accounting or on the accrual basis of accounting. Table 3-8 outlines the differences between the 2 methodologies.

Accrual accounting is better for financial reporting purposes in that it provides a more accurate depiction as to how the company is operating; however, most medical entities manage finances on the cash basis. However, when medical practices compile their profit and loss summaries, they are not usually based solely on a cash basis, but rather on the modified cash basis. This is because some items, such as depreciation or amortization, must be recognized yet have no relationship to cash (ie, a practice will never write a check to depreciation or amortization, but they are legitimate financial operations). Most of the items are true representations of actual cash-in (revenue) and cash-out (expenses) except for those few items (ie, depreciation, amortization). Thus it is not actually a statement of cash flow or a true profit and loss statement but rather a modified profit and loss statement under the cash basis.

When determining which return will be measured, it is generally accepted that a return comparable to the entity in question will be used. Therefore, when looking at a medical practice one will usually consider earnings after taxes (EAT) when valuing equity and EBITDA or EBIT when valuing invested capital.

TABLE 3-8

Cash vs Accrual Accounting

	Cash Accounting	**Accrual Accounting**
Revenue	Recognized when it is collected	Recognized when it is *earned* or the service has been completed
Expenses	Recognized when charged	Recognized when activity related to the expense has been incurred

The methods used to calculate EAT (equity) and EBITDA and EBIT are illustrated in Table 3-9.

The relationship between the various returns are highlighted as the anticipated benefits of the company. In the case of a medical practice, generally, EAT will be used, though, if it is determined that the appraiser will be focusing on the invested capital of the company, then another return will be used. In order to actually calculate the net cash flow (NCF) to equity or the NCF to IC, the steps as outlined in Table 3-10 are applied.

Discount Rates

In its most basic form, the DCF method can be broken down into 2 parts, the return and the rate that will be used to capitalize the return. "A present value discount rate is an 'opportunity cost', that is, the expected rate of return . . . that an investor would have to give up by investing in the subject investment—instead of an available alternative investments that are comparable in terms of risk and other investments characteristics."[11]

Other terms that are often used to describe the discount rate include the following:

- *Opportunity cost of capital*
- *Required rate of return*
- *Weighted average cost of capital*

But while rates may be referred to with different terms, they share the following characteristics[12]:

- Rates are market determined.
- Rates vary with time, even with the same investment.

TABLE 3-9

Calculation of EBITDA, EBIT, and EAT

Invested Capital	
Net adjusted income after taxes	*$89,458*
Plus depreciation	$75,895
Plus amortization	$14,500
Plus interest	$75,898
Plus taxes (40%)	$58,972
EBITDA	**$314,723**
Less depreciation	$75,898
Less amortization	$14,500
Less taxes	$58,972
EBIT	**$165,356**

Equity	
Net adjusted income after taxes	*$89,458*
Plus depreciation	$75,895
Plus amortization	$14,500
EAT	**$179,853**

TABLE 3-10

Calculations of NCF to Equity and NCF to IC

Net Cash Flow to Equity	
EAT (including D&A)	$179,853
Less capital expenditures*	$18,292
Less increase in working capital†	$23,977
Plus increase in long-term debt‡	$27,469
NCF to Equity	**$165,053**

Net Cash Flow to Invested Capital	
EBIAT	$179,853
Less capital expenditures*	$18,292
Less increase in working capital†	$23,977
Plus interest expense §	$45,539
NCF to IC	**$183,123**

*Based on the practice's balance sheet (Appendix A), change in equipment of $632,371 in 2002 to $650,663 in 2003.

†Based on the change in the practice's working capital per the balance sheet, of $214,423 to $238,400 from 2002 to 2003 (respectively).

‡Based on the practice's balance sheet of $482,657 to $510,126 from 2002 to 2003 (respectively).

§The practice's interest expense, per 2003 income statement, net of taxes (assumed 40%).

- Rates incorporate inflationary expectations.
- Rates accommodate general market risk and must be adjusted for risk specific to the asset or right being appraised.
- Rates are based on the alternative investment yields.
- Rates depend on the nature of the future 'income' stream.

While rates as a whole may vary considerably, that which must remain constant is the way in which discount rates are applied. In the previous section, it was noted that a number of different returns could be utilized. However, what must be considered is that for each individual return used, the discount rate applied will be different. Thus, the appraiser must never forget the importance of ensuring that the "discount rate developed must be matched conceptually and empirically to the definition of economic income (ie, return, anticipated benefit, etc) being discounted."[13]

Capital Asset Pricing Model

One of the most reliable approaches used to determine the discount rate for a particular investment is the capital asset pricing model (CAPM). This model can be exhibited as follows:

$$R_e = R_{rf} + \text{Beta} \ (R_m - R_{rf})$$

Where:

R_e: This is referred to as the expected rate of return, required rate of return, or the discount rate. This is the rate that is being calculated.

R_{rf}:   This is the risk-free rate. This rate is associated with an investment that has no risk. (Absolutely no one thing has no risk; however, for purposes of this process, this rate will be referred to as *risk free*.) This rate of return is usually associated with an investment instrument such as US Treasury obligations. This would be the rate that an investor would expect as the minimum payment for their investment. The valuation community is often at odds as to what constitutes this figure, some lean toward short-term government bills or intermediate-term government notes, though for purposes of this analysis, it has been assumed that the most pure risk-free rate is found in long-term government bonds. This risk-free rate can be found in any number of financial journals. The source most often used to determine this figure is *The Wall Street Journal* (either the print version or the Web site at www.wallstreetjournal.com).

Beta: This is known as the measure of systematic risk. The simple definition of beta is the risk of the investment (or a similar investment) compared to the risk of the market. The market as a whole has a beta of 1.0, and the risk of the company is based on this standard. Therefore, an investment that has a beta of .80 would be considered less risky than the market. Correspondingly, an investment with a beta of 1.2 would be considered more risky than the market. (In some instances, a company may exhibit a beta of a negative number. This means that the beta is counter-cyclical to the market.) When there are enough comparables to perform a market analysis, the beta for the subject company may be derived from these sources (eg, the median beta for all guideline companies), such as Standard & Poor's *Compustat*[14]; however, if it has been determined that there are not enough market comparables to perform a market analysis, it may be appropriate to use the information provided by Ibbotson's *Stocks, Bonds, Bills & Inflation*,[15] which will provide a market beta.

$R_m - R_{rf}$:   This is referred to as the *equity risk premium*. This is the level of risk that an investor can expect over and above the risk-free premium. This is the amount that an investor must be paid to invest money in another investment other than a risk-free investment. The figures used to calculate the equity risk premium are usually determined from Ibbotson's.

The CAPM provides a sound benchmark, but it only compares returns to the risks of the market, and this may be somewhat flawed in that it assumes that only market risk is compensated. Companies most certainly incur additional risks. This is why an additional term, referred to as *alpha*, has been added to the CAPM. When alpha is added, the formula appears as such:

$$R_e = R_{rf} + \text{Beta } (R_m - R_{rf}) + \text{Alpha}$$

This is often referred to as the *build-up method* of the CAPM. Alpha is defined as:

Alpha: The measure of unsystematic risk in the market. While beta measured the systematic risk pertaining to an investment, alpha looks at more company- and market-specific data including size, specific market risks, as well as others.

When determining a company's size premium, an analyst may consider the variance of the company's industry (eg, a small company) versus the market: $R_s - R_m$ (such data can be found in source material such as Ibbotson's). This is the necessary return that a normal investor would require to invest in an equity whose size is smaller than the market. In addition to size, one must also consider other pertinent data that would only be found for the subject company. A medical practice may include (but not be limited to) any of the following items related both to the field of medicine and the practice's local market, such as:

- General uncertainty of health care
- Increase in malpractice premiums
- Decrease in reimbursement
- Increased competition
- Dependency on referrals
- Solid patient base*
- Solid provider base*
- Solid management base*

This data is often a compilation of both verifiable market data, in combination with the appraiser's best judgment. This is where the appraiser's knowledge of the company, the industry in which it operates, and valuation fundamentals are put to the test. Without an intimate understanding of all of these issues, the appraiser cannot expect to adequately determine this value.

Consider the following example for the subject company practice being valued. (Note: The information used in this context is available from daily postings in *The Wall Street Journal* and through other resources such as can be found at www.ibbotson.com.):

$$R_{rf}^{(1)} = 4.86$$
$$\text{Beta}^{(2)} = .77$$
$$R_m^{(3)} = 10.65$$
$$\text{Alpha}^{(4)} = 11.00$$

----

*In determining the alpha for the CAPM formula, one must consider both the positives and the negatives associated with the company. All of the viable scenarios should be considered, weighed, and netted against one another in order to properly determine the net discount (or premium) for the specific market risk. In the case of the asterisks, these would be considered positives for the subject company.

[1] Based on the 20+ year Treasury Bond

[2] As calculated from Ibbotson Associates Cost of Capital 2002 Yearbook for SIC Code 8, unlevered beta for Small Composite

[3] As calculated from Ibbotson Associates Cost of Capital 2002 Yearbook for SIC Code 8, S&P 500 Index[16]

[4] Based on various factors determined from the specific analysis of the practice and the practice's specific market

The following illustrates the placement of values into the formula and the calculations that occur to arrive at the equity discount rate:

$$R_e = R_{rf} + \text{Beta}\ (R_m - R_{rf}) + \text{Alpha}$$

$$R_e = 4.86 + .77\ (10.65 - 4.86) + 11.00$$

$$R_e = 4.86 + .77\ (5.79) + 11.00$$

$$R_e = 4.86 + 4.46 + 11.00$$

$$R_e = 20.32$$

Based on these calculations, an equity discount rate of 20.32 has been calculated. Some appraisers will choose to round this figure (20, in this instance), though there is no evidence for or against this. For purposes of this analysis, the discount rate will remain as 20.32 (ie, rounded to 2 decimal places or the hundredths position).

Growth

In most cases of performing a valuation, an appraiser will be valuing a company that is expected to continue operating for some period in the future. And one would hope that as this business continues it will grow, whether by increasing its revenues or decreasing its expenses, or some combination of both. All businesses wish to grow at least equal to the rate of inflation (which would actually be considered no growth), but most companies that wish to remain in business—certainly all public companies—desire to grow much more. Value is the present value of all future cash flows. As noted, it is the goal for every business to grow at some rate; therefore, a growth rate must be applied to the return that is being considered. In the case of the subject company, it has been determined that the practice's normalized EAT will grow at a constant rate of 4% throughout the next 3 years (see Table 3-11).

The growth rate can be determined in a number of ways. It can be based on historical growth with considerations for the future performance of the practice. It can be based on recommendations from the company's management. Likely, most companies will perform an annual budget (and sometimes a longer-term budget, though this is difficult in smaller practices where unknowns abound) that can be used to help calculate an effective growth rate. Although, especially in the case of a smaller practice, an appraiser will have to base the growth rate on a combination of issues including guidance from management and his or her own best estimates. Again, the importance of selecting an appraiser with detailed knowledge of the industry and the specific market is paramount to this process.

TABLE 3-11

Estimate Growth Rate

	2003	2004	2005	2006
Growth	(base)	4.0%	4.0%	4.0%
NCF to Equity	$165,053	$171,655	$178,521	$185,662

Using growth estimates provided by management is often an excellent tool and can be very helpful, especially in markets where the appraiser is less than familiar with the topic. However, the appraiser must place a "reality check" on the estimates and consider if they are really attainable. For instance, an analyst may consider such things as reimbursement in the area (ie, has it been increasing or declining in the past years?), the market for patients (ie, are there enough patients to sustain the growth projected?), competition (ie, is the market saturated with providers?), and the future of the practice (ie, will the practice be recruiting new providers?). Also, an analyst will want to consider how the practice has grown in the past. For example, if a practice has grown only 2% in the last 5 years and management is projecting 20% growth for the next year, this would be something to consider. This example should not be discounted because if the practice receives a new exclusive contract to perform all of the procedures for one particular insurance company, this could substantially increase business. Conversely, in some cases, management may just inflate potential growth knowing its implication on the value of the practice.

Incorporating these well-thought-out questions with the management's projections (if it is even available) will generally provide a fair, representative view of the company's growth potential.

Value Calculation

Now that an appropriate rate of return has been calculated and the return for the next 3 years (the model period) is forecasted, information can be put into action to calculate the value of the practice. The basic formula that is used to determine the value of the entity is as follows:

$$\overbrace{}^{\text{Cash Flows}} \qquad \overbrace{}^{\text{Terminal Value}}$$

$$PV = \Sigma E_T/(1 + R_e)^T \quad + \quad [E_{T+1}/(1 + R_e)^T]/(R_e - g)$$

Where:

E_1 *through* E_n: Expected return used to base the value

R_e: Discount rate

T: Number of periods

g: Long-term growth rate

$(R_e - g)$:   Capitalization rate

The model for the practice will be calculated as follows:

$$PV = \frac{\$171{,}655}{(1.2032)^1} + \frac{\$178{,}521}{(1.2032)^2} + \frac{\$185{,}662}{(1.2032)^3} + \left[\frac{185{,}662/(1.2032)^3}{(.2032\text{-}2.5)} \right]$$

$$PV = \$142{,}665 + \$123{,}313 + \$106{,}586 + \$598{,}139$$

$$PV = \$970{,}703$$

Based on the analysis, an equity value for the practice of $970,703 has been calculated.

Weighted Average Cost of Capital

Throughout this valuation process, the 2 areas of focus have been the valuation of the equity and the valuation of the IC (ie, debt plus equity). In the DCF method, the value of the practice's equity has been determined; however, in order to determine the value of the practice's IC, a method referred to as the *weighted average cost of capital* (WACC) must be applied.

This value is not typically used in the valuation of smaller medical practices because it requires an entity to have a certain amount of debt. Smaller medical practices generally have little to no debt. However, this method could be very useful in determining the value of a larger business or a newly formed company where a larger amount of debt on record may exist. Because the WACC is not typically used in the valuation of medical practices, does not mean that it should never be considered.

The formula used to calculate a firm's WACC is as follows:

$$\text{WACC} = (k_e \times W_e) + (k_d\,[1 - t] \times W_d)$$

Where:

k_e: The firm's cost of equity

k_d: The firm's cost of debt

W_e: The percentage of equity capital

W_d: The percentage of debt capital (interest bearing debt)

t: Effective tax rate

Using the value of the firm's equity in conjunction with the market value of the firm's debt (per the balance sheet), these figures are applied in Table 3-12.

Based upon the previous calculation, the practice's WACC will be 10.796.

When determining the WACC, the same return is not used as in the equity model, rather, the return is somewhat modified (see Table 3-13), though the same growth rate will be applied as in the equity model.

Once the return that is being measured has been determined and the WACC rate calculated, these 2 factors will be used to calculate the value of the practice using the same present value formula as in the equity model. As follows:

TABLE 3-12

Equity vs Market Value of Invested Capital (MVIC)

Classification	Amount	Percent (Weight)	Cost of Capital	WACC
Firm's debt	$510,126	.602	x 4.5*	2.709
Firm's equity	$337,933	.398	x 20.32	8.087
WACC				**10.796**

*This was determined by multiplying the practice's cost of capital, 7.5% (interest rate) for its debt by (1-*t*). The *t* was assumed to be 40%.

TABLE 3-13

Net Cash Flow to Invested Capital

	2003	2004	2005	2006
Growth	(base)	4.0%	4.0%	4.0%
NCF to IC	$183,123	$190,448	$198,066	$205,988

$$PV = \frac{\$190{,}448}{(1.10796)^1} + \frac{\$198{,}066}{(1.10796)^2} + \frac{\$205{,}988}{(1.10796)^3} + \left[\frac{\$205{,}988/(1.10796)^3}{(.10796 - 0.25)}\right]$$

$$PV = \$190{,}448 + \$161{,}344 + \$151{,}451 + \$1{,}825{,}591$$

$$PV = \$2{,}328{,}834$$

This represents a total of the equity, debt, and, in this case, the final value that is being sought. In order to complete the process, the following step must be completed:

Value of IC	$2,328,834
Less debt	− $510,126
Value of equity	**$1,818,708**

Clearly, this value calculates a different value with a variance of approximately $848,005, which raises the point of which methodology is better. In these circumstances, the calculating would be left to the discretion of the appraiser, but the value of the equity utilizing the DCF model is probably a more accurate calculation of the practice's value.

Marketability and Ownership

Once the various values of the practice have been determined and the appraiser has determined the most appropriate value to be applied, one final step must take place. Because certain market information has been used that is derived from minority-owned, highly marketable shares of ownership, both a premium and a discount must be applied to account for these items.

Various studies have analyzed ad nauseam in order to better understand the appropriate premiums and discounts that should be applied to valuations utilizing this market data. Studies have determined figures ranging from 5% to 20% to as high as 50% for discounts and premiums in some cases. Obviously, there is some sway in determining the appropriate figures to be applied. An appraiser should examine the various studies and determine which one, if any, is the most applicable and employ it accordingly.

Final Step

The final step in calculating the value of an entity, regardless of the approach, is for the appraiser to apply a reality check to the final figure. This check is a very simple and important step in calculating the value of an entity.

In order to complete this step, the appraiser must review the work that has been completed and look at the valuation not in each individual calculation but as a whole. The final value that is calculated via the DCF methodology is considered and compared to other market values (if available). For instance, if the value under the equity approach for the subject practice is calculated at a value of $5,000,000, the appraiser would likely want to reconsider the value. Every step may have been applied appropriately and the appropriate data used to calculate the discount rate, but a value of $5 million for such an entity is not very likely. In this case, the appraiser would likely want to go back and reconsider some of his or her assumptions. First, the appraiser should consider all completed financial calculations. Was the restated salary comparable to what the practice is actually paid? Instead of the median salary, perhaps the 75th percentile should be used? Did a simple miscalculation of the numbers lead to the exorbitant value? Once the appraiser has checked all of the calculations, he or she should review the more subjective calculations. Did the market data used to calculate the discount rate appropriately apply in this scenario? Were the other premiums and discounts not appropriate? Were the growth rate and other assumptions applied accurately? Answers to any number of these questions could be the source for an unreal value.

Completion of this reality check is by far the most necessary step prior to finalization of the valuation process. If this step is not completed and the appraiser presents a clearly overstated, indefensible value, this could damage the appraiser's credibility with the client and within the valuation community.

CONCLUSION

The heart of this valuation process is the actual computation of the value. Numerous methodologies can be used to calculate the value of a medical practice or other entity, and the importance of a competent appraiser is stressed throughout.

Although various methodologies to value an entity can be employed, the knowledge of the appraiser and the standard of value that is being sought will dictate which basis of value to apply. The income approach is the one most recognized by the IRS; however, in certain situations, this may or may not be applicable (eg, a company that has no intangible value or a company that has invested a large amount of funds in real equipment).

The depth of information that could have been conveyed in this chapter is absolutely fathomless, especially if the focus had not been primarily on medical entities. In order to provide a better understanding of the key methodologies and the processes by which they are calculated, much of the detail that these methodologies are based upon (especially in the income methodology) have been avoided. Every detail regarding business valuation has not been covered, but instead, a general understanding and know-how of what comprises a medical entity valuation has been provided.

NOTES

1. American Society of Appraisers. Introduction to Business Valuation, Part 1. In: *Principles of Valuation: Business Valuation Student Manual*, BV 201. Herndon, Va: American Society of Appraisers; 2002:7.

2. Ibid., 66.

3. Ibid., 75.

4. Ibid., 76.

5. Ibid., 79–80.

6. Ibid., 67.

7. Fishman J. The problem with rules of thumb: the valuation of closely held entities [Commentary]. *Fairshake*. December 1984:4.

8. Appraisal Standards Board. *Uniform Standards of Professional Appraisal Practice*. 2002 ed. Gaithersburg, Md: The Appraisal Foundation; 2002.

9. American Society of Appraisers, 90.

10. Ibid., 92.

11. Ibid., 159.

12. Ibid., 21–31.

13. Ibid., 159.

14. www.compustat.com

15. www.ibbotson.com

16. www.ibbotson.com

chapter 4

Valuation Guidelines

Now that the basic concepts of medical practice appraisal (which is information applicable to various health care entities), the valuation process itself, and the specific methods have been reviewed, a few extraneous items are discussed in this chapter. In addition, research and operations of the valuation process are covered. A valuation data checklist, a useful tool to ensure that the appraiser is working with the essential information to reach a relevant valuation of the practice, is also included.

MULTIPLES, RATIOS, AND RULES OF THUMB

Multiples and ratios are integral in the valuation process. Two of the most important factors in the income approach are multiples, which include the capitalization rate and the discount rate. Some of the key financial benchmarks are ratios, like the debt ratio and current ratio, among others. Financial evaluation of a business requires a full appreciation and comprehension of multiples and ratios.

Another ratio that is often used in the valuation industry is that of rules of thumb. *Rules of thumb* are industry standards expressed as a ratio of some number; for a medical practice, this could be the number of active patients to net collections, or active charts to net collections. For the most part, these are useful ratios to compare one entity to the subject entity as is done using the market approach.

The problem with strictly using ratios is that just looking at the ratio tells you nothing about the entities being compared. What if the rules of thumb are taken from a random group of practices and no consideration is given for qualitative factors (such as the type and size) or details related to the practice? What if the practices are taken from an area that has a higher level of capitated patients? This situation would likely result in a high number of active patients to only average income and the ratio being used would be the number of active patients to total collections. Furthermore, what if the ratios consist of only highly specialized practices where active patients will be relatively low and collections should be considerably high?

Ratios and multiples have their place in the valuation process, but they must be applied in the appropriate context and with consideration. Rules of thumb are nothing more than blind ratios that can cause more problems than they solve.

Most times those who are not informed of the valuation process will make comments like, "Can I just apply a multiple to find the value?" They question why it takes so long to determine a practice's value when they believe they can gather a few multiples from the Internet, briefly review the income statement, make some calculations, apply the multiple, and arrive at the value.

Often, clients will make comments like, "I heard that medical practices are selling at 6 times income," and will wonder why their value is so low. This is a common misconception that appraisers have to fight, and the appraiser has to educate the client on what is appropriate. Multiples and ratios have their place in the valuation process but not as rules of thumb.

APPLICATION OF VALUATION METHODOLOGIES

Chapters 2 and 3 review a number of the valuation methodologies. Applicable methodologies can be used to determine the value of a medical entity. In the case of valuation, each project should be considered in its own right and the appropriate standard should be applied.

Accordingly, the appraiser should be knowledgeable in all fields of valuation science and know which methodology and standard should be applied and when it should be applied. This is especially the case when valuations in the health care field can have far-reaching implications. Because of the role that the government plays in health care, a great deal of attention is paid to transactions that take place. This is also the case because of the high preponderance of not-for-profit entities that exist in the health care marketplace.

An appraiser should be familiar with these issues and know how they can potentially affect the valuation and any transfer of ownership. For instance, if a hospital is purchasing a medical practice, then it is not appropriate to include the revenue generated by the practitioners for the hospital and compensate them directly for that revenue. That would violate any number of laws related to Stark and anti-kickback statutes (see Chapter 6). As such, a valuation methodology that considers this revenue may not be appropriate in this instance; an appraiser should be aware of this.

In addition, health care entities can be highly dynamic and very unstable. This is even more the case in small practices. Physicians and staff come and go and, in most markets, there is high portability for patients between providers (in this case, HMOs may actually benefit the provider where patients are limited in who they can and cannot see). All of these factors must be considered in the valuation process. This is why the entity should be valued for its future operations, not its past.

The market approach is a highly regarded method for valuing organizations, but should a practice receive a multiple of 3 times collections if 2 physicians just left and there is no plan to replace them? If those collections cannot be assured in the future, why should the multiple be applied to them?

This is another reason that historical valuation methodologies, such as the asset-based approach to valuation, are less reliable. They consider the historical operations rather than the future operations. With the rapidly changing health care industry, how can these be an applicable method of valuation when they only look at the past, not the future?

In the past, a number of appraisers relied on the replacement methodology for valuing the goodwill (ie, the intangible portion) of medical practices. Chapter 2 provides an in-depth description of this valuation methodology; essentially, it considers the price that it would take to "recreate" the current practice, as is. The applicators of this methodology contended that if a hospital was going to purchase a medical practice, then it should be valued at the price that it would take for that hospital to start that exact same medical practice. This always benefits the seller (the practice, in this case) because there is substantial investment to starting a medical practice: paying recruiting fees, initializing lines of credit to cover the periods of no-cash flow, providing income guarantees, etc.[*]

However, does this represent the true fair market value of the practice, the amount that would result from the exchanging of property between a, "willing buyer and willing seller"?[1] It would appear not. This methodology does not consider the future value (ie, what may happen in the future as compared to what happened in the past).

Even though this methodology was heavily relied upon in the past, its applicability has since been outdated and, in most cases, will not provide an appraiser with a clear determinant of fair market value of an ongoing entity.

RESEARCH THROUGH THE INTERNET

The Internet has become a vital tool in improving the dissemination of information. In the appraisal industry, information is king. As quick as a couple of clicks on the Internet (and one credit card number), the information that is available is virtually unlimited. Any number of databases, studies, and other critical information can all be found on the Internet. The Internet has in fact proven to be an invaluable tool in the appraisal process.

In the days before the Internet, the research that was required to complete a valuation would take hours upon hours of library, telephone, and interview work to ensure that nothing was missed. Now, information can readily be transferred from point to point, and reams of data that once was too costly to even maintain can now be stored in electronic format and downloaded by even the most computer illiterate person. Programs like Adobe Acrobat®, Microsoft Word®, Microsoft Excel®, and a myriad of others being used on the Internet have made the collection, the storage, the exchange, and (most importantly) the ability to understand and interpret that information easier than ever before.

In addition to making information more available, the Internet has also been made more current. In the past, companies that published key market data would usually do so in large-volume books that were purchased on an annual basis. This information usually had a 1-year lag time (eg, while it was published in 1999, it was generally based on 1998 data). Certainly this information is useful—at the

---

[*] Additional discussion of this topic can be found in the AMA Press publication titled *Starting a Medical Practice*, Second Edition, by Jeffery P. Daigrepont (2003).

time, it was the only way of providing that information—but year-old data is not the timeliest of information. The Internet, however, has, for the most part, done away with the need for this time lag. Information can be updated on a regular basis as needed or as events occur. The need for the 1-year lag time is gone, and information can (and should) be updated almost on a real-time basis.

The ease of application on the Internet is 2-fold. Not only does it make information more available, but it also allows anyone with a computer, a telephone line, and an opinion to become a self-appointed "expert." With such a simple medium (ie, the Internet) with which to work, virtually anyone can post information. Thus, the appraiser must take responsibility to gain an understanding of what is reasonable and realistic versus that which is meaningless.

Sure, someone may have performed a study of initial public offerings (IPO) that concluded that there is a 110% premium for control ownership, but does this mean that it is an accurate study and that the results were properly reached? What if the study was performed by Bob's Valuation and Pest Control? And what if Bob's study considered just 2 stocks over a period of 25 years? This may not be the best study to reference when applying the rationale for a control premium.

Just because an article or study is posted on the Internet does not mean that there is any validity to it or that it bears any shred of truth. Most credible information is cited in a number of different places. For example, if an obscure review about a study performed 30 years prior was cited in passing and no mention of that review can be found elsewhere, be leery. Likewise, if, while doing research on an issue, a specific study is constantly cited, chances are that that study is valid. Regardless, one should always verify information.

Another unfortunate outcome of Internet research is the amount of useless information that is provided. For every page of useful information found on the Internet, 20 pages will probably be useless information. Whether it is supporting documentation or useless information, the researcher must be able to sift through everything and determine what is necessary and what is not. Internet research should be done quickly and proficiently so that fees are not in question (see the appraisal fees section of Chapter 5). If the majority of the researcher's time is spent sorting through information rather than truly applying it, then the time spent on the project will exceed budget.

Appendix B lists a number of Web sites and other informational sources that can be useful for research purposes.

OPERATIONS ASSESSMENT

In order to perform a full valuation of an entity, especially in the health care industry, the appraiser must have a detailed knowledge of that entity's operations. The operations have a direct influence on the entity's future earnings and how they will be affected in the future. The operational review and its depth will be commensurate with the size of the entity. For example, a smaller medical practice can be reviewed relatively quickly. But a large hospital or nursing home may take considerably more time to review.

Another reason to procure an appraiser with thorough knowledge in health care is because operations play a large part in determining future earnings. Knowledge and understanding about how health care entities work, which can be quite different from the operations of other service entities, can provide a level of insight that a regular appraiser may not bring.

Operations are key to understanding the subject company, and the operations assessment is basically a broad overview of the entity's operations. If the appraiser is qualified to provide such services, this is often an ideal time for the entity to conduct a detailed operational study. Operations should be reviewed on a regular basis, conducted at the minimum of every 5 years, to ensure that operations are running well. Some larger companies may even have their own internal audit team that periodically reviews both financial and operational issues. Unfortunately, it is likely that smaller organizations cannot afford to allocate their own people, much less have a dedicated team, to review the organization's operations. Plus, when an organization allocates internal personnel, the reviewer may not have the knowledge to understand the broad range of issues or may be more reluctant to report mismanagement to the boss.

A detailed outside review can avert many of these issues. In addition, if an appraisal is being completed (either mutually or separately) by one organization that is looking to invest in or purchase all or a portion of another entity, they should have the utmost concern for how that organization operates.

For example, if an orthopedic practice is considering the purchase of another practice, the orthopedic practice should be knowledgeable about the financial operations, billing and collections, personnel staffing and benefits, etc. This is true with all service companies, but it is especially true within the health care industry because the services and the operations that go on to produce those services are the underlying foundation to the whole business. These are issues that transcend a normal appraisal and move into what is commonly referred to as a detailed operational review.

A detailed operational review may consist of (but is not limited to) a review of any one of the following issues:

- Personnel review
- Revenue cycle analysis
- Internal controls and procedures
- Management information systems review
- Patient management analysis
- Regulatory and compliance analysis
- Facility review
- Demographic analysis

All of these issues are in addition to the detailed financial review that is completed in order to perform an appraisal. In fact, some companies will have an appraisal completed on a regular basis to evaluate the financial stability of the organization. This is an ideal time to perform a detailed operational review.

VALUATION DATA CHECKLIST

Regardless of whether a detailed operations assessment will be completed, the appraiser requires a staggering amount of information to complete the valuation. Again, this exact information and the detail that is sought will be based upon the extent of the valuation and the size of the entity. However, an example of a data requisition for the full valuation of a typical-sized medical practice has been provided in Appendix A. This information will vary based on the size of the entity and the scope of the review.

CONCLUSION

This chapter covers general items that are essential to the valuation process but not in the same categories with the previous topics of review. *Multiples, ratios, rules of thumb*, and *valuation methodologies* are more than merely jargon used by the competent appraiser. These terms are indeed essential components of the project. This chapter also delivers some useful information about resources available for gaining the necessary background to attain the needed ratios, multiples, and rules of thumb. This is the practical chapter that helps the appraiser get the job done for the client and helps the client accept the steps that are being taken with a measure of understanding.

NOTE

1.   Internal Revenue Service. Revenue Ruling 59–60.

Managing the Appraiser-Client Relationship

Chapters 1 through 4 discuss each component of the valuation and valuation process. The process includes engaging an appraiser to calculate the values and considering the various standards and approaches that are available to complete the process. One aspect of the process that has yet to be discussed, however, is the interaction between the appraiser and the client.

When it comes to assessing the value of a business entity, few books address the interaction between the client and the appraiser. Nevertheless, this topic is an integral part of the process. This aspect is not found in most texts because relationships are subjective. Generally, positive interaction between the client and the appraiser is learned "on the job" or conveyed to new appraisers from those who are more experienced. Positive interaction is as integral to the assignment as calculating an accurate discount rate.

Chapter 5 reviews some of the key areas that go beyond the actual valuation process and trend into more of the relationship phase of the project.

MANAGING THE APPRAISER

Managing the appraisal process begins with basic knowledge of the appraiser and the associated fees. In order to better work with the appraiser, it is helpful to understand that sometimes "gray" area that develops between the professional and personal relationship between the appraiser and client.

Know the Appraiser

A vast number of people offer appraisal services and represent themselves as business appraisers. The field includes those who specialize in everything from widgets to wing nuts, and each field has its own methodologies and approaches that are more accepted than others.

As discussed in Chapter 3, the income approach is identified as one of the most effective approaches for valuing a medical practice. However, an appraiser that specializes in real estate will probably never utilize a discounted cash flow (DCF) or the income approach because a business valuation and real estate valuation are 2 separate schools of value and utilize many varying techniques.

Small firms will usually specialize in only 1 business field, whereas, the larger firms will cover numerous fields and *practices*, as they are termed, within their appraisal department. Larger firms likely have an employee pool large enough to span the wide range of knowledge that is required in such an operation.

Generally, when selecting an appraiser, it is important to find one that exhibits the skills and knowledge specific to the industry under consideration. Appraiser firms are companies that specialize in doing business valuations in varying fields, whether it is a 1-physician family practice or a multi-billion dollar a year potato chip manufacturer. The important point is not the size of the firm. Large or small, when it comes right down to it, it is likely that the same processes and methodologies will be applied.

The first step should be to find a qualified appraiser or firm that knows the ins and outs of a medical practice, surgery center, or medical facility. An appraiser who knows business may not necessarily understand the business of medicine. For this reason, someone that is knowledgeable **both** in health care **and** the appraiser field should be considered.

The field of medicine has its specialists and subspecialists (eg, a general surgeon and an orthopedic surgeon). Just like some physicians, some appraisers subspecialize. While some appraisers only value medical entities, some will have experience limited to one specialty (eg, surgery centers, radiology practices). This may be fine, or it may be better to select an appraiser that has a broader viewpoint. It might be a mistake to engage someone so focused on one field that he/she does not have a broad scope of what goes on in the rest of the medical industry. Typically, a qualified appraisal firm in the health care field will have adequate knowledge of any specialty.

When considering hiring an appraiser, a client should seek the recommendation of professional organizations, such as the American Medical Association, Southern Medical Association, and other specialty societies and associations. These organizations can provide a list of competent appraisal firms. Also consider references from legitimate valuation-specific sources, such as the American Society of Appraisers. Clients might also seek referrals from colleagues who have recently had an appraisal conducted.

Nevertheless, a referral does not ensure that the recommended firm or appraiser is best suited or most qualified, especially in the medical field. Likewise, one colleague's appraiser may not be appropriate or qualified for all types of practices. For example, an appraiser may have received a high rating from a practice because the medical practice was valued at 10 times earnings before interest, taxes, depreciation, and amortization (EBITDA) rather than because he/she was competent and qualified. And who knows, maybe the appraiser valued that practice at 10 times EBITDA because of incompetence.

Remember, a recommendation from a firm or an association does not mean they are competent or qualified to value a practice. Unqualified appraisers and firms outnumber qualified ones; therefore, when hiring a firm to do an appraisal, a client should research possible candidates. Questions to ask an appraiser or firm include the following:

- Does the firm have any professional certifications?
- How long has the firm been doing appraisals?
- On average, how many appraisals does the firm do each year, etc?

It is appropriate to probe a little further to discover what the appraisal firm knows about appraisals in the medical field. Some such questions may include the following:

- How would a relative value unit (RVU)-based compensation system affect the value?
- How have the recent Health Insurance Portability and Accountability Act (HIPAA) laws affected medical valuations?
- How does coding affect the valuation calculations, etc?

Going into detailed clinical issues does not mean that the appraisal firm does not know anything about health care appraisals. More than likely, it means the firm does not know anything about the clinical side of health care (and there is a difference). Ultimately, an appraisal firm that knows about RVUs, HIPAA, and Current Procedural Terminology (CPT®) will likely be well versed in the health care field. Likewise, the practice's certified public accountant (CPA), although knowledgeable in the fields of finance and accounting, may not be a skilled business appraiser. A client, firm, or association referral of an appraisal professional should not be accompanied by a referral fee. Whether a firm provided competent appraisal services can often be swayed by a referral fee.

Appraisal Fees

Most appraisers will set hourly fees within the proposal for services. The full valuation is quoted and hourly rates are typically held to the quoted price, regardless of extra hours that may be incurred.

All sizes of companies, whether large or small, need appraisers, and the appraiser should be priced accordingly. First, it must be understood that for a full, in-depth appraisal to be completed, a significant amount of due diligence has to be done. The completion of an appraisal is anything but the entering of a few numbers into a spreadsheet model. If the appraisal is to be properly conducted, the practice should be willing to make the investment in a competent appraiser.

The magnitude of work that goes into an appraisal for a smaller medical practice is not as substantial as that for a larger practice or hospital. Furthermore, if an appraiser that specializes in the health care field is chosen, the appraisal can proceed with greater ease as the person is more knowledgeable in the field and is much better equipped to handle the research end of the appraisal.

If an appraisal is to be properly conducted, be ready to make the necessary investment. Beware of the appraiser that promises a detailed appraisal in 5 to 10 hours or who only needs to review a copy of the company's financials in order to provide "a number" for a full appraisal. Granted, if the practice only requires that calculations be made, then perhaps supplying financials is all that is warranted. But caution is advised. The level of the practice's involvement will be commensurate to the project being completed.

No set amount of hours can be given as a benchmark as they will change with every entity. As long as the proper due diligence is outlined in the proposal and completed and all of the approaches are considered, the client should reasonably be able to determine if the hours that are estimated are appropriate for the size of the entity.

Much like the appraiser that agrees to complete an appraisal in a very short period of time, the appraiser that seems to "move in" and never leave should also be avoided. Many larger practices pay exorbitant fees for professional service and knowledge. However, charging high fees and assigning a small army of consultants to the project does not ensure that a large firm will be any more effective than a smaller appraisal firm.

MANAGING THE CLIENT

Every story has 2 sides. The client must make sure the appraiser does not abuse privileges. The appraiser should maintain a level of professionalism that ensures the client does not abuse the business relationship.

Fair and Independent

The appraiser must be aware that many times the owner of a practice, especially a small medical practice, has dedicated his or her life to the practice. In such cases, the appraiser must not allow the client to influence any decisions or outcomes.

Consider an appraisal being completed on a physician's majority ownership of a thriving surgery center for legal purposes (eg, divorce). While this physician may be honest and full of integrity, at the same time, he or she may try to influence the final value of that ownership. An appraiser has to rise above any kind of undue influence and stand up to the client that tries to compromise the appraiser's professionalism. This is especially true in today's business environment where business ethics commonly take on a whole new meaning.

As big as it may seem, the appraisal community, much less the medical appraisal community, is small, and bad news travels fast. If a consultant or firm is proven to be less than trustworthy in any of their dealings, legal actions may occur if any damage is committed. This would be the least of the firm's worries. The appraiser should remain fair and independent and without reproach. The consultant/firm's reputation and ability to attract future clients relies on unwavering honesty and integrity, not just doing what the client wants.

Although unfortunate, clients are not going to be happy all of the time. This is especially true for medical practice appraisals, and doubly true for small medical practice appraisals. Physicians often dedicated their lives to their practice and when it comes time to appraise the value of that practice, if the value falls short of expectations, the appraiser is the person relaying the bad news. Even if the practice had a considerable amount of value based on the appraisal (eg,

$200,000), but they were under the impression that the medical practice should be selling closer to 10 times revenue (eg, closer to $1 million), the appraiser's value cause some serious disagreements between the client and the appraiser.

If the appraiser follows the rules and standards set forth, there may be some subjectivity that allows for disagreement (eg, the calculation of the discount rate under the income approach, the application of discounts and premiums), but with the proper due diligence and reasonable assumption outcomes, subjective decisions should be more than defendable.

If there was a legitimate error that led to a mistake (eg, a considerable onetime expense that went unnoticed), the appraiser's fair and independent nature should not be impugned because of the oversight. It is difficult for an appraiser to learn everything about any entity, its history, and what comprises its operations with only a few days on-site, so it is likely that some misinterpretations may occur, and if they do, the appropriate adjustments should be made.

Knowledge Is Power

The appraiser should provide detailed knowledge and understanding of all appraisal issues. They should be well adept in accounting, finance, and the industry in which the subject company operates. Unfortunately, there are only a few universities that offer degrees in business appraisal (though there are schools with said classes). Therefore, much of the information that is learned is either on-the-job training or from extended education.

Extended education not only includes higher education (eg, masters, doctorate) but also other accreditation programs that specialize in business appraisal. In fact, these other accreditation programs are some of the most useful areas in which to receive continued education. Additional accreditation may be received from organizations such as the following:

■ American Society of Appraisers (ASA)
■ Institute of Business Appraisers
■ American Institute of Certified Public Accountants
■ Canadian Institute of Chartered Business Appraisers
■ National Association of Certified Valuation Analysts

Any person that is choosing to go into the business appraisal field should strongly consider seeking accreditation with one of these associations.

Most people do not attend accreditation classes immediately after completing college. Instead, many spend a few years gaining experience before they make their career choice and choose the appraisal field. Thus, it may occur that someone who has not started the accreditation process is performing appraisals, which is fine as long as they are supervised by someone with the knowledge and understanding of the issues. There are many mundane financial analyses and research that must be completed in an appraisal process, and as long as the appraiser is competent and understands the process, there is no reason for concern. In fact, many of the larger firms conduct business in this manner.

Regardless of who is completing the work, the person who is responsible for and signs off on the report (see Chapter 2) should have a detailed knowledge and understanding of the appraisal process and know how the report was completed. Rarely will it occur that both sides of the appraisal (ie, the seller and the buyer) will be completely happy with the proposed number. Most of the time the seller will think the price is inordinately low and the buyer will think it much too high. This is human dynamics.

When an appraisal is completed, the appraiser has to be able to answer all of the questions with certainty and clarity and know everything about how the value was calculated. If not, this may cast doubt on the appraiser and the legitimacy of the report.

It is imperative that the appraiser be skilled and knowledgeable in all areas of business appraisal. For example, if, during a presentation meeting, the appraiser is asked why a certain methodology under the asset-based approach was not applied, the answer to this question must be thoughtfully and concisely forthcoming. If there is question as to why a premium or discount was applied via a market valuation, the appraiser should be able to answer that question, citing one of the many supporting studies to bolster the reply.

Again, there is subjectivity that does go into every report, but if the appraiser can cite evidence and supporting documentation as to why or why not an approach was applied, the final calculation will be all the more bulletproof.

Expert Witness

First and foremost it must be said that not everyone is cut out to be an expert witness. Attorneys and appraisers are often teamed together or against one another to defend an appraisal. Although work as an expert witness is challenging, it can often be very daunting when up against an attorney whose soul purpose is to prove a case against the appraiser.

As previously noted, often times the 2 parties in an appraisal will disagree as to the value of the entity in question. In a normal appraisal case, this situation may occur; but in expert witness work, this is almost always the case. As fate will have it, lawyers do not normally get involved if something is going well, and if an appraiser is being called as an expert witness, there is almost total certainty that someone is pushing from the other side of the table. Whether it is the attorney trying to punch holes in the appraisal or another appraiser hired by the other side, the validity of the appraisal is in question.

In this case, the other side (ie, the attorney or appraiser) is going to do everything possible to find even the smallest detail that may have been missed. And when or if that detail is found, it could be challenging to defend the project. Even that smallest detail can be enough to defeat the entire appraisal. If this does happen, the client should be wary of the attorneys on both sides of the table. Though a competent attorney would typically find any mistakes before they became a problem.

Because of the challenges, some appraisers refuse to do expert witness projects. The best rule of thumb for appraisers choosing to get involved as an expert witness is to not go into a project unprepared. When working as an expert witness in the appraisal field, the appraiser must be intimately knowledgeable with regard to *all* issues of business appraisal, including the ability to cite resources, back up and verify all information, and pinpoint every method's applicability in the business appraisal. The appraiser should not only be informed of business appraisal standards but also of statutory and common law. If the appraisal's methods include some level of subjectivity, being able to tell the opposing attorney that even the courts recognize that ". . . valuation is necessarily an approximation and a matter of judgment, rather than of mathematics. . . ."[1] Also, knowing something about the attorney's world will make operating in it a lot less painful.

CONCLUSION

Whether client or appraiser, both roles have duties and responsibilities to fulfill. The client has the obligation to choose the appropriate appraiser and do the research to make sure that the person/firm they choose is competent and understands business appraisal.

The client should focus on a firm that will provide the services that are needed within a reasonable fee structure. Most firms will provide fees on an at-risk basis, but it is the client's role to understand the value of investing in a competent appraiser. Do not expect to get a full, adequately prepared document for just a few thousand dollars. There is a required level of due diligence that the appraiser has to perform, and if someone promises to complete the work for a lower price, then it is likely that the finished product will be of a lower quality.

The client must be up front with the appraiser. Although every appraiser would like the final product to be joyfully accepted, the appraiser should not put up with undue influence from the client. Likewise, a client should not get half way through a project, change the deliverable, and then expect the appraiser to not increase the cost.

As the client has obligations, so does the appraiser. If a deliverable is promised, the appraiser is obligated to provide it. If the appraiser has priced the project too low, corners should not be cut on the final report.

Professionals that choose to pursue a career in the appraisal business should learn every aspect of the business. Receiving the proper accreditations should be a goal. Maintaining knowledge on new happenings within the industry and continuing education should always be a priority.

NOTE

1. *Davis v Commissioner*, 110 TC 530,554 (1998). Citing from *Hamm v Commissioner*, 325 F2d 940.

Regulations in the Appraisal of Health Care Enterprises

Laws that apply to health care entities that do not apply to other industries must be considered when conducting an appraisal of a health care entity. This is one reason why it is important to select an appraiser that has the knowledge and scope of understanding of the regulations in the health care environment. Knowing the ins and outs of health care regulation is imperative to not only deriving the effective value (eg, has the entity historically been in violation of one particular regulation that may decrease the future value of the entity), but also the implications of the appraisal. Thus, the appraiser has a dual role: to be knowledgeable of the multitude of financial and valuation guidelines, and to understand the sundry health care regulations and how they coincide with the financial issues.

Health care is one of the most highly regulated industries in the nation. Medicare (administered by the federal government) and Medicaid (administered by state governments) account for a disproportionate figure in terms of expenditures when related to other industries. This makes it easy to understand why there is so much concern over money being prudently spent.

Non-profit organizations (NPOs) are an additional aspect that play a large role in the delivery of health care across the country. Numerous hospitals, health care organizations, practices, and other related entities are structured as NPOs. Subsequently, they are subject to additional regulation, both from the Internal Revenue Service and the Office of Inspector General (OIG).

This chapter presents a brief overview of significant health care regulatory matters and how they affect both the value of an organization and its potential valuation process. Discussed in this chapter are some of the more specific legislation, such as the Stark laws, anti-kickback laws, and newer rules, such as the Health Insurance Portability and Accountability Act (HIPAA). Although the health care appraiser should be familiar with these ordinances, they should not serve as the full and final authority on health care regulation.

INTERNAL REVENUE SERVICE

Involvement of governmental agencies in health care and the presence of the Internal Revenue Service (IRS), relating to not-for-profit, tax-exempt status, command a review of the regulatory issues specific to appraisals. Not-for-profit (generally tax exempt) health care providers who are involved in acquisitions must understand and follow accepted guidelines for valuation and purchase of physician practices. This section presents a general overview, summarizing the regulatory issues and laws and their direct effect on the independent appraiser and the client.

Inurement

The IRS holds that an organization that is exempt from income taxes under IRS Code Section 501(c)(3) and applicable state statutes is prohibited from entering into transactions that allow any of its earnings to *inure* to the benefit of a private shareholder or individual. Furthermore, regulations supporting this IRS Code Section provide that an exempt charitable organization may not be organized or operated for the benefit of private interests. This proscription is generally called the *private benefit doctrine*. Private inurement may take many forms and may include the physician compensation portion of the acquisition/employment, particularly incentives. In examining a transaction between a not-for-profit entity and an individual (ie, a physician), consider inurement in light of the expectation of cash flows and purchase price.

A hospital may seek to improve or protect its market share by purchasing a physician practice. The hospital takes this action to ensure a continued referral base or to prevent competitive hospitals from intruding into its market share. While this exercise is legal, to adhere to the private benefit doctrine, the purchase price for the practice must not exceed fair market value. If it does, charges of inurement can be alleged.

Compensation factors can also affect inurement. If pay is based on a percentage of profits of the physician's practice, or if the hospital otherwise solicits or induces referrals or admissions, inurement can result. Therefore, it is important to avoid potential inurement when determining fair market value of a practice.

The valuation of a practice in light of potential inurement requires understanding of the nature of cash flows and application of acceptable, meticulous methods for valuation. The independent appraiser must impartially approach this project, applying acceptable standards to the valuation.

Medicare and Medicaid Anti-Kickback Statute

Consequences can result if a hospital (tax-exempt or for-profit) engages in activities or makes financial arrangements that violate statutes established for Medicare and Medicaid patients. Infractions by a tax-exempt hospital can jeopardize its exempt status and its ability to serve Medicare and Medicaid patients. Likewise, losing its ability to serve Medicare and Medicaid patients negatively affects a for-profit hospital. The issue of Medicare and Medicaid fraud and abuse exposes health care providers to situations that can threaten their existence. In practice appraisal, if the acquisition or joint venture with physicians is in breach of prescribed regulations, both the physicians and hospital may be subject to serious penalties and prohibitions.

FEDERAL HEALTH CARE REGULATIONS

The activity level of mergers and acquisitions occurring in health care is generating increased scrutiny by agencies that are responsible for regulating the industry. These probes are designed to eliminate potential conflicts of interest resulting from physicians and other health care providers who obtain undue financial gain from questionable referral activity. The federal government has written legislation as an attempt to define and regulate questionable referral practices. This legislation, commonly called Stark I and Stark II, is briefly summarized in the following paragraphs.

Stark I

In 1991, the Health Care Financing Administration (HCFA), which is now called the Centers for Medicare and Medicaid Services (CMS), published regulations for the Ethics in Patients Referrals Act. This act was labeled Stark I because of its author, United States Representative Fortney "Pete" Stark (D), California. Stark's Act prohibited physician referrals of Medicare patients to clinical laboratories where the physicians had ongoing financial involvement. The financial involvement or relationship was defined as "any ownership or investment interest (including both equity and debt) or any compensation arrangement."

Stark I was enacted through the Consolidated Omnibus Budget Reconciliation Act of 1990 and published late in 1991. Limited in its scope, the primary objective of this law is the prevention of physician referrals to clinical laboratories in which they have financial relationships. Many practicing physicians operating private laboratories as an adjunct to their medical practice experienced financial repercussions from this law. However, subsequent Stark legislation rendered widespread financial consequences on practicing physicians.

A review of the Stark laws indicates that Stark I altered the value of clinical laboratories receiving substantial income from referrals of Medicare patients by their physician owners. During the late 1980s and early 1990s, many transactions ensued as physicians divested themselves of ownership interests in laboratories. Independent appraisers were required to consider projected decline in future operating revenues and profits previously generated from the laboratory operations. Using acceptable methods of valuing physician practices, many calculations are based on the prospect of future earnings. Now, a definitive stream of revenue and profits (ie, the revenue from laboratory operations) ceased. Stark I significantly reduced the value of practices. Subsequently, transactions occurred at high prices reflecting adjusted asset values. The historically high profit levels and associated intangible value that existed before Stark I were generally ignored.

Stark II

The Consolidated Omnibus Budget Reconciliation Act of 1993 authorized an extension of the initial provisions of Stark I. As of January 1, 1995, Stark II prohibited physicians and physician family members with financial relationships to an organization from referring a patient to that organization for clinical laboratory services and to any of 10 additional "designated health services." Distinguishing itself from Stark I, Stark II restricted referrals of Medicaid patients in addition to Medicare patients.

With Stark II becoming effective January 1, 1995, the primary objective of this law was to preclude physicians from the Medicare and Medicaid referrals. Primarily, this pertained to referrals to clinical laboratories and the other "designated health services." These were designed to be preclusions from organizations with which physicians maintain financial relationships. Such "designated health services" included the following:

1. Physical therapy
2. Occupational therapy
3. Radiology or other diagnostic
4. Radiation therapy
5. Durable medical equipment (DME)
6. Parenteral and enteral nutrients, equipment, and supplies
7. Prosthetics, orthotics, and prosthetic devices
8. Home health care
9. Outpatient prescription drugs
10. Inpatient and outpatient hospital services

As a list, the preceding is comprehensive, but number 10 alone—inpatient and outpatient hospital services—brings immense implications for the operations of physicians and to the valuation of physician practices.

Comparable to Stark I, Stark II precipitated an immediate and negative effect on the value of health care entities providing the denoted services. Those generating a large portion of their revenue from the referral of Medicare and Medicaid patients also would be dramatically stricken.

Therefore, an appraisal analysis performed for these entities requires the following:

■ Quantifying historical revenues and profits resulting from such referral streams related to prohibited referral practices
■ Estimate of normalized future operating revenues and profits resulting from the exclusion of prohibited referral streams from future operations
■ Analysis of additional risks attributable to the operating entity and the overall future economic viability resulting from the immediate loss of significant revenue sources

For many corporations and partnerships, significant revenue and profit are directly attributable to their ownership of entities that are providing ancillary medical services (many qualifying as "designated health services"). The appraiser must consider how compliance with Stark II affects those operations in reviewing partnerships and corporations. If the physicians have historically referred a high level of Medicare and/or Medicaid patients to the "designated health service," Stark II negatively influences the valuation total. In short, loss of referral streams reduces the value of the entity.

Integrated Delivery System Implications

Integrated delivery systems (IDS) throughout the United States face an interesting dilemma regarding Stark II. The health care industry at large is pressed to develop a system that provides increased access and lower costs. In response, IDSs have flourished across the nation. Stark II regulations, however, appear to present a conflicting point of view from the concept of integrated delivery. By restricting referral patterns between physicians and inpatient and outpatient hospital services, Stark II seems to be "anti-integration" and "anti-managed care." It prohibits otherwise-apparent natural health care relationships (ie, "designated health services").

Often in IDSs, funds flow between hospital and physician providers, with the possibility of creating an indirect "compensation relationship" between them. For example, in a full-risk capitation arrangement, a hospital provider and one or more physician groups in the integrated network may share capitation funds. According to Stark II, they have likely created a prohibited referral pattern. Because of referrals to the hospital for inpatient and outpatient services, the physician receives compensation from the hospital.

As managed care organizations (MCOs) operate primarily as health maintenance organizations (HMOs), they focus on reducing costs by controlling access to providers and services. Providers participating with MCOs through an IDS find it inherently unappealing and financially imprudent to overutilize physician services. Yet, Stark II presents an opposite view. Philosophically, the Stark Bill conflicts with managed care's trend for formation of IDSs.

Compensation Exceptions, Personal Service Arrangements

Stark II contains many exceptions, with the most significant relating to compensation. These exceptions are considered in the following list:

- *Compensation exceptions, personal service arrangements.* These exceptions represent compensation for incentive provisions in physician service contracts. Legislation allows these exceptions if payment is determined in advance and in accord with the fair market value of service performed. The agreeing parties must arrange for payment without regard to referral volume, for a minimum period of 1 year, and covering all services provided by the physician. Agreements are acceptable if the services do not include promotion of business arrangements that violate any state or federal law.
- *Physician recruitment.* The hospital may pay a physician to relocate to the hospital if they do not require that the physician refer patients to that hospital and the compensation is not in any way tied to the number of referrals.
- *Group practice arrangements.* An arrangement where a group of physicians provides services to patients who are, in turn, billed by the hospital must have begun before December 19, 1989. This

only applies to inpatient services that most of the group provides. Compensation must conform to fair market value for the services and be commercially reasonable, even with no referral implications.

- *Physician payments.* These must be payments made by a physician to a laboratory for clinical services or to an entity as compensation for the fair market value for services provided by an entity.

- *Remuneration unrelated to designated health services.* This represents payment by a hospital to a physician for non-designated health services and is allowable.

- *Isolated transactions.* These represent onetime sale of property that qualifies if they satisfy the requirements set forth for *bona fide* employment relationships.

- *Bona fide employment relationships.* This represents employment that must be for specific ascertainable services. Compensation must be at the fair market value for the services provided and be a part of an agreement that is commercially reasonable, even if they anticipate no referrals.

- *Office space or equipment rental.* This requires a lease term of at least 1 year in writing, and signed by the parties. It must specify the covered space and/or equipment. The lease rate must be set in advance and may not be based on the volume of referrals that are generated between the parties and must be commercially reasonable.

Stark III

Stark III legislation is currently under way. This is a broad and sweeping bill aiming at extending the current referral bands to all patients, whatever payer. Furthermore, this legislation anticipates including all ancillary services. With the shift of the US Congress to a Republican majority in 1995, Congress has reduced, or placed on extended hold, the Stark III legislation.

Summary of Stark Legislation

Stark legislation has caused sweeping changes in health care and, in addition, uncertainty and questions of the legality of certain transactions. Overall, the Stark legislation attempts to prohibit any provider transactions that are illegal referrals of patients by the physician. The true objectives of all Stark legislation are to curb the physician referral practices based on perceived conflicts of interest and to prevent overutilization of identified medical services.

Due to the complicated nature of this legislation and its implications, health care entities that are contemplating buying, selling, or contracting should quickly consult qualified legal counsel and experienced valuation experts. This should preclude costly misunderstandings about the legality of certain business practices and their bearing on valuation.

INTERPRETATION OF VALUATION PROTOCOLS BY THE IRS

The IRS has interest in the accuracy of valuations of medical practices. With so many hospitals operating as tax-exempt organizations, the tax implications are significant if hospitals purchase medical practices at anything other than fair market value. Specifically, if the transaction is completed at something greater than fair market value, the IRS would legitimately question the health care entity's tax-exempt status.

Favorable exemption letters issued by the IRS and based upon Section 501(c)(3) of the Internal Revenue Code typically include the following language: "Applicant represents that all assets required will be at or below fair market value (FMV) and will be the result of independent appraisals and arm's length negotiations."[1]

Clearly, the continuation of tax-exempt status relies heavily on the applicant's sound documentation and arm's length appraisals of all business enterprises that it anticipates purchasing. Critical issues are whether appraisals are correctly performed by outsiders who are totally independent.

Tax Exemption

As previously stated, many health care organizations have received tax-exempt status under Section 501(c)(3) of the Internal Revenue Code. These organizations must be operated exclusively for charitable purposes with no part of their net earnings inuring to the benefit of any private shareholder or individual. Typically, the *community benefit standard* prevails. This focuses on factors that suggest that the operation of a hospital benefits the community rather than serving private interest. Often, the intent for a tax-exempt hospital, for example, is that it is controlled by a board composed of independent persons, has an open medical staff, is active and accessible, serves everyone without regard to ability to pay, and treats all patients able to pay for their care, including both Medicare and Medicaid patients. Conclusively, then, the hospital operates to serve the public rather than private interests.

To continue tax-exempt status, health care providers such as hospitals must continuously avoid 3 major situations. These are private benefit, private inurement, and violation of fraud and abuse laws. The remainder of this chapter will discuss these situations.

Private Benefit

A health care organization, such as a hospital, cannot be organized or operated exclusively for charitable purposes unless it serves public interests. Therefore, to meet the stipulations of Section 501(c)(3) of the Internal Revenue Code, an organization must establish that it has not organized or operated for the benefit of private interest, specifically certain designated individuals. These individuals could include, for example, the founder of the entity and his or her immediate family, shareholders of the organization, or persons controlled directly or indirectly by such private interest. Private shareholders are individuals who have a personal and private interest in the activities of the organization.

The private benefit prohibition applies to all physicians in a medical group who sell assets to a tax-exempt organization and all physicians subsequently performing professional services for that organization. Benefits to the physicians must be balanced against benefits to the public.

The tax-exempt organization is allowed to provide benefits to private individuals or persons who are not members of a charitable class, provided those benefits are incidental, both quantitatively and qualitatively. In other words, organizations can benefit the public without necessarily benefiting certain private individuals. The community can receive the same services without unnecessarily benefiting the seller if the purchasing health care organization uses an after-tax cash flow analysis. Therefore, if they employ a pretax cash flow analysis, private benefit to the medical group derived from the inflated sales of assets may be significant.

To be *quantitatively incidental*, any private benefit must be insignificant, "measured in context of overall public benefit conferred by the activity." This will depend on the reason behind the benefit and whether the advantages provided are greater than necessary to accomplish the exempt purpose. The reason for using a pretax cash flow analysis is to further private interest through payment of more than fair market value. It provides greater-than-necessary benefits to the private interest to accomplish exempt purposes. The private benefit from use of the pretax analysis would be considered quantitatively substantial as measured in context of overall public benefit to the community. This overpayment would therefore be a serious negative component in making a determination of an organization's community benefit.

It is also relevant to remember that private benefit may involve anyone, including an unrelated seller's assets to an exempt organization. An organization's conferral of benefit on disinterested persons can cause it to serve a private interest and jeopardize tax-exempt status.

Private Inurement

Private inurement generally relates to persons whose particular relationship with an organization creates an opportunity to influence or perhaps control its activities. Such "insider" identity may cause a less-than-free market environment for transactions.

Private inurement is more restricted in concept than private benefit. Inurement generally will not be found without an outsider; conversely, private benefit may involve anyone. In addition, while certain lower degrees of private benefit are acceptable if it is incidental to the accomplishment of exempt purposes, Section 501(c)(3) of the Internal Revenue Code strictly prohibits inurement. Therefore, an essential issue of determination is whether a physician in such a transaction is an insider.

The IRS recognizes the fact that certain key employees of an exempt organization have the potential to exert inside influence. It follows, then, that physicians in a medical group providing services for an IDS, either as employees or under a professional services contract, may exert considerable influence over the organization. This insider status would require the IRS to examine the potential for inurement and substantial private benefit.

Inurement is not present if an organization can demonstrate that its relationships with potential insider physicians are at arm's length and that the physicians have no realistic opportunity to exert inside influence. The inurement regulations do not prevent the payment of reasonable compensation for goods and services for the purchase of assets at fair market value. Again, this is within the acceptable parameters of such transactions that assume that the business enterprise value (BEV) is based upon fair market value. Conversely, inurement is aimed at preventing dividend-like distributions of charitable assets or expenditures to benefit a private interest.

Fraud and Abuse

Hospital management and directors are keenly aware that they must align with well-established primary and specialty medical groups. If not, their hospitals may not be positioned to take advantage of the expansion of managed care. Hospitals, sensing a threat to their very survival, may be enticed to pay a premium price to acquire a medical practice. They may intentionally purchase the medical group's assets at a premium, while maintaining the appearance of arm's length negotiations. In reality, they may have allowed independent appraisals to be contrived to secure physician referrals for the hospital.

Federal anti-kickback restrictions prohibit compensation or any remuneration in return for referral of Medicare and Medicaid patients. Section 1128 B[42 U.S.C. 1320 (b)(1)]a of the Social Security Act states restrictions as follows[2]:

> Whoever knowingly and willfully solicits or receives (or offers or pays) any remuneration (including any kickbacks, bribes, or rebates), directly or indirectly, overtly or covertly, in cash or in kind
>
> a. In return for referring an individual to a person for the furnishing or arranging of any item or service for which payment may be made in whole or in part under the federal health care program, or
>
> b. In return for purchasing, leasing, ordering, or arranging for or recommending purchasing, leasing, or ordering any good, facility, service, or item for which payment may be made whole or in part under the federal health care program, shall be guilty of a felony and upon conviction thereof, shall be fined not more than $25,000 or imprisoned for not more than 5 years, or both.

In addition to the monetary fine and imprisonment, convicted individuals or entities are also precluded from participation with any other governmental payment programs.

Those activities prohibited by this federal anti-kickback statute are quite broad. The prohibition applies to cash payments made in return for direct physician referrals. Subsequent litigation has also ensued in application of the statute to situations where the receipt of cash payments directly or indirectly induces a referral. Literal interpretation may have superceded Congress' intentions by affording the potential for the prohibition to apply to customary activities. Recognizing the ambiguity of the laws, Congress instructed the Secretary of Health and Human Services (HHS) to issue regulations specifying certain safe harbors. These *safe harbors* are payment practices that will not be subject to criminal prosecution under the federal statute and will not provide a basis for exclusion for participation in government-sponsored programs. The Office of Inspector General (OIG) of HHS has published regulations outlining certain safe harbors under the federal anti-kickback statute.

The safe harbor regulations contained provisions for remuneration paid in connection with the sale of a physician's practice. The preamble to the regulations acknowledges that hospitals and other health care organizations acquire physician practices to secure a stream of referrals, and they pay more money for the practice than would otherwise be available in the marketplace. In these circumstances, the additional compensation reflects the value of referrals and would constitute an illegal payment. Because of this abuse, the safe harbor provision contained in the regulations relates only to the sale of practices between practitioners, where the seller will not be in a position to make referrals to the purchaser after 1 year from the date of sale.

A 1992 letter from the OIG of HHS to the Technical Assistant (Health Care Industries) expressed concern that some acquisitions of assets from medical groups may violate the Medicare and Medicaid anti-kickback statute. If an acquisition is illegal, an organization may jeopardize its exemption under Section 501(c)(3) of the Internal Revenue Code. At issue are intangible assets that relate to the continuation of treatment of the selling practice's patients. Examples are amounts paid for goodwill, value of an ongoing business, covenants not to compete, exclusive dealing arrangements, patient lists or records, etc. Where the courts and the OIG have definitively determined the illegality of particular remuneration, the IRS will not deny or revoke exemption. However, the IRS must be aware of this potential problem. The IRS currently includes the following language in favorable exemption determination letters[3]:

> This ruling is conditioned upon your not violating the Federal Anti-kickback restrictions contained in section 1128(b) of the Social Security Act, 42 U.S.C. code section 1320a-7b(b)(1) and (2) which prohibit the payment of remuneration in return for the referral of Medicare or Medicaid patients. We express no opinion about whether your planned purchase of a private group medical practice or your subsequent payment for physician services complies with the provisions.

Summary of IRS Valuation Protocols

Governmental regulations as they relate to the physician practice valuation have briefly been introduced in this chapter. With most integrated delivery systems consisting of primarily tax-exempt components, the IRS is obligated to see that transactions involving tax-exempt organizations do not create profits that would be subject to taxation. Furthermore, state and federal programs, such as Medicare and Medicaid, represent a significant portion of the health care dollar. Therefore, these programs are concerned about arm's length transactions and unfair practices that illicitly influence business through additional referrals.

HIPAA'S INFLUENCE ON VALUE

HIPAA will likely not affect the value of a health care entity nor the manner in which the value is completed. However, it is highly advisable that an appraiser be knowledgeable of its basic premise and its key points.

HIPAA, whose scope seems to have increased since it was first proposed, primarily covers the transfer of electronic and other information via electronic and non-electronic means. Again, its original scope primarily applied to larger health care entities, insurance providers, and health care providers, and protecting patient information as it is transferred via these 3 intermediaries. Congress originally proposed such legislation when the introduction of electronic communication of patient information became more commonplace in these intermediaries, yet it has been somewhat slow to be fully developed and implemented.

An appraiser of a health care enterprise does not have to be an expert in the HIPAA regulations, but he or she must know how it affects the entity being valued and how the value is conducted.

With regard to how the value is conducted, the appraiser must understand that certain information is considered protected patient information (PPI). If PPI is being conveyed from the health care entity to the appraiser by electronic means for any reason, the appraiser must ensure that the appropriate measures are in place for the PPI to remain confidential. In addition, the professional should have some sort of privacy policy (see Chapter 2) in place to ensure that these measures have been implemented and will take place.

Secondly, and probably foremost when considering the value of an organization, the appraiser must be knowledgeable of the HIPAA guidelines and what they require of each entity. If the entity does not have an effective HIPAA plan in place and is not adhering to the regulations, then this must be considered as a factor in the valuation of the entity.

Perhaps because of their reluctance to implement a plan, the entity may face reprimands from the government that may place a future financial burden on the entity. Additionally, if the entity is without a plan, it may face future charges attributable to the implementation. Whatever the case, the appraiser must know how the HIPAA regulations will affect the entity being valued.

CONCLUSION

The information in this chapter provides a brief overview of the myriad of governmental regulations that the appraiser must consider when conducting an appraisal of a health care business entity. The question is not so much how these regulations affect the value—though this is something that must be considered—but how they affect the valuation process.

The valuation of health care entities requires not only the knowledge of valuation and financial guidelines and procedures, but also an understanding of various laws and regulations that are specific to health care entities. When performing these valuations, it is often beneficial to the appraiser to be familiar with these laws and regulations, such as a professional that specializes in the field of health care.

NOTES

1.   Section Code 501(c)(3) of the Internal Revenue Code.

2.   Social Security Administration. Criminal Penalties for Acts Involving Federal Health Care Programs. Section 1128B.[42 U.S.C. 1320(b)(1)]. Available at: www.ssa.gov/OP_Home/ssact/title11/1128B.htm. Accessed October 2, 2003.

3.   Internal Revenue Service. Taxpayer: Panama City Free Clinic, Inc [Primary Source Material: IRS Exemption Rulings]. *TaxCore*. March 25, 2003. Available at: http://subscript.bna.com/SAMPLES/txc.nsf/0/eca32586f03eab4185256cf300808c07?open. Accessed September 25, 2003.

chapter 7

Preparing the Practice for Maximum Value

This chapter offers practical guidance for optimizing the value of a medical practice in preparation for a sale. Attaining peak value is the goal of an owner of any business. Medical practice ownership is no different, especially in preparation for a sales transaction. Enacting sound business practices will assure improved operating results and subsequently increase the value of the practice.

The following initiatives should be an ongoing part of the practice's business strategy, regardless of whether the owner intends to sell. Keeping a practice running in top-notch condition could be compared to maintaining real estate in tip-top shape in order to capitalize on its value. In the meantime, the owner enjoys optimum returns and benefits in the duration of ownership and is always prepared to sell. Preparing the practice for valuation involves several areas of management, including the following:

- Growth in revenue and productivity
- Management and control of expenses
- Strategic planning and future initiatives

GROWTH IN REVENUE AND PRODUCTIVITY THROUGH REIMBURSEMENT STRATEGIES

Obtaining maximum reimbursement from payers for a medical practice is the most important issue for the long-term economic viability—if not survivability—of a practice. One way a practice can prepare to maximize its value is to establish a productivity and revenue base, but this entails some internal assessment. A good place to start is with the practice's payer mix, the forms of reimbursement, and the associated strategies. Next, a review of the practice's fee schedules—an exercise that should be done periodically—is conducted. The review is followed by an assessment of the internal productivity standards, referral patterns, and compensation incentives. Last, the stability of the practice is considered in terms of transfer of ownership, staffing, and other factors of strength.

Evaluating the Payer Mix

Preparing the practice for maximization of value involves the consideration of the payer mix (a frequently used term for the make-up of categories of payers). Payer mix can include self-pay, traditional or indemnity insurance, managed care plans (eg, health maintenance organization [HMO], preferred provider organization [PPO], capitated, fee-for-service), and federal- and state-funded programs, such as Medicare and Medicaid. The mix of payers is immensely important to the practice, and depending upon the type of practice, the payer mix can cause great variances in operating results. For example, a practice weighted heavily with Medicare patients (where professional fees are significantly discounted) will not compare favorably in profit margins and ensuing *value* with a practice bound by fewer contractual discounts. An internal medicine practice with a payer mix that approximates one-half or greater Medicare patients compared with one with one-third or less presumably will operate at lower margins, better cash flows, and lower valuation totals.

In a contrasting example, a practice that performs a great deal of elective procedures and services may not depend so heavily on third-party reimbursements, with the presumption that these patients will be expected to pay according to the physician's fee schedule. Margins, therefore, are much greater. This concept can be applied to any of the valuation methodologies to enhance practice value.

Obtaining maximum reimbursement relies largely on developing a strategy to enhance the payer mix. A profitable practice must maintain a desirable payer mix that includes nondiscounted fees. In a nutshell, the more discounted fees, the lower the resulting valuation of the practice.

The question becomes, "How will the practice moderate levels of payer mix?" Many variables influence the answer, including the following:

- The age of the physicians and their practice
- The age of physicians' patients
- Strategic alliances (as a source for patient referrals)
- The marketing strategies for the practice
- Managed care involvement
- The geographic setting (eg, urban vs rural)

The following example highlights a case where the physician's practice profile has a significant relationship with the payer mix:

> A physician in his early 60s has practiced at the same location for more than 25 years. His patient base has not changed over time (ie, he has minimal managed care involvement). This is typical of an internal medicine practice where the majority of patients were pre-Medicare age at the outset. More than likely, the physician's patient base has aged with him, and now most of the patients are "Medicare."

The ratio of Medicare patients must be considered in the valuation process as a significant factor in its operating results. To maximize practice value, the physician can pursue several options. In this example, the physician can do very little at this stage in his career to alter the payer mix (ie, he will want to maintain his current patients). However, even in this phase, he can improve his payer ratio by aggressively marketing to younger patients. He may achieve this through direct involvement with managed care companies. Assistance is available also for patient referrals from the hospitals where he serves as an active member of the medical staff.

As a physician sees these trends developing, he or she can modify the payer mix. Changes are not effortless, however, and depending upon the specialty can be difficult. By the nature of their specialty, internists are apt to see a high percentage of Medicare patients.

Developing a balanced payer mix enhances practice value for the future. Not only does this augment the value for a prospective purchaser, but it also positively reflects to a managed care company reviewing and credentialing physicians for its panels. Conversely, a physician can work hard to achieve a more favorable payer mix with uncertain results, or he can do nothing and be assured of the outcome.

Knowledge and appreciation for the payer mix gives the owner a realistic view for the potential attraction and value of the practice and the time it may need to prepare for the sale. It takes time to make changes and they only occur through a long-term process. Realistically, changes in payer mix cannot start in the same year that the physician prepares the practice for valuation and subsequent sale. The cycle takes 3 to 5 years prior to the sale, and even at that, a lot will depend upon the practice's competitive position in the community, number and reputation of the providers, facilities and location, and many other considerations.

The practice owner that needs to sell within the next several years will have an opportunity to enhance value through a concerted marketing strategy and managed care campaign. The physician that needs to sell immediately, however, will have less time to achieve shifts in the payer mix, and if the valuation must be done soon, the practice's value must be considered essentially at its current level. The independent appraiser, who must be fair and objective, will be reluctant to assume significant changes in payer mix or margins in reimbursement after the sale. Payer-mix trends are a major consideration; if the trends indicate little, if any, improvements in reimbursement in the future, the appraiser must draw conclusions accordingly.

Fee Schedule Analysis

The setting of the physician's fees and the subsequent collections influence the definitive value of the practice. The aim of every medical practice is to set fees for each service that are reasonable, fair, and close to what third-party payers (ie, Medicare/Medicaid, managed care companies, and insurance companies) will pay. A common misconception is that the practice has no control over reimbursement and that payers pay what they want. However, practices do not have to accept contracts that are not beneficial to them. As previously discussed, it is essential to have a balance of payers to benefit the practice. Likewise, it is necessary for a practice to not only ensure that fees have been set high enough to capture the existing indemnity insurance coverage, but also to identify the costs of providing their services. Practices need to cover costs and, like any other business, to make a profit.

With an efficient internal revenue cycle in place, an effective strategy toward the external revenue cycle, and an aggressive, yet reasonable approach to establishing its fee schedule, a practice may indeed be successful in improving reimbursement.

It is important to review and evaluate fee schedules at least annually with the following objectives:

- Establish a reasonable fee for the practice
- Compare reimbursement to cost/by payer
- Sell that fee schedule to managed care organizations and patients

Medical practices typically develop fee schedules based on 1 or more of the following:

- **Historical charges.**   An easy way to update fees, this method assumes that the fee schedule was adequate in the first place. The disadvantage is that it has no scientific or analytical basis.
- **Prevailing market rates.**   This approach ensures that the practice is not gouging self-pay patients compared to other practices in the community and will provide payers with a basis for payment. It does not, however, take into consideration the difference in cost structure of the comparable practice. The disadvantage is that the term *health care market* can involve many variables and specialty nuances influenced by payer volatility and reimbursement methods. Also, it is difficult to assign market prevailing rates due to scarcity of accurate market data and legal constraints on fee-setting initiatives.
- **Percentage of Medicare fee schedule.**   An effective method is to apply a percentage to the current Medicare fee schedule, which works well as long as the practice's percentage is higher than the highest payer. The drawback is that it does not lend itself to effective contract negotiations, and the fact that rates vary significantly within specialties and codes, with some Medicare rates being more acceptable than others.
- **Cost to deliver services.**   The most viable, yet most difficult, method is to derive fees based on cost to deliver service. The ability to determine this number depends on the level of sophistication of data accumulation and the reviewer's discernment.

If the physician and/or practice administrator is unqualified to complete a fee schedule review, an outside consultant should be contracted to conduct a review. Sophisticated methods are in use to compare fees with allowable reimbursements for various payers, including government, private insurance, and managed care companies. A suitable starting place is a review of insurance explanation of benefits (EOB) statements. Sample commercial insurance EOBs may be easily obtained. The EOB document shows the physician's fees billed for services rendered and the amount the insurance company approved for payment. In addition, the EOB also shows the copayment and deductible paid by the patient. Because commercial or indemnity insurers do not pay physicians on a contracted fee basis, there is opportunity for consideration of usual, customary, and reasonable charges.

Begin the fee schedule analysis by reviewing each Current Procedural Terminology (CPT®) code to assess fees in relationship to usual, customary, and reasonable charges set by commercial insurance companies. If it is determined that the physician has not reached the usual, customary, and reasonable threshold, there is opportunity for additional reimbursement and increases in the fee structure. This results in an increase in fees collected and enhancement of the value of the practice.

Medicare

Medicare's physician fee schedule uses a relative value system known as the resource based relative value system (RBRVS). RBRVS is a system for measuring physician input to medical services for the purpose of calculating a physician fee schedule. The relative value of each service is the sum of relative value units (RVUs) presenting physician work, practice expenses, and the cost of malpractice insurance.

The Medicare physician fee schedule amounts are adjusted to reflect the variation in practice costs from area to area. A geographic practice cost index (GPCI) has been established for every Medicare payment locality for each of the 3 components of a procedure's RVU (ie, the RVUs for work, practice expense, and malpractice). The GPCIs are applied in the calculation of a fee schedule payment amount by multiplying the RVU for each component times the GPCI for that component.

To understand how the CMS determines Medicare physician fee payments, look at the payment formula for 2003, following:

$$\text{2003 pricing amount} = \left[\left(\text{Work RVU} \times \text{Work GPCI}\right) + \left(\text{Practice Expense RVU} \times \text{Practice Expense GPCI}\right) + \left(\text{Malpractice RVU} \times \text{Malpractice GPCI}\right)\right] \times \text{Conversion Factor}$$

For example:

$$99213 = [(0.67 \times 1.006) + (0.69 \times 1.059) + (0.03 \times 0.935)] \times 36.7856$$
$$= \$52.71$$

The conversion factor is the multiplier that transforms relative values into payment amounts.

Managed Care Implications

Managed care is described as a system of health care services being provided and financed to a specified group of recipients. In addition, managed care plans involve alliances of health care providers intended to produce the following results:

- Reduce health care costs
- Encourage preventive health care
- Effectively utilize health care resources

The best known forms of managed care today are PPOs and HMOs. Managed care and various forms of reimbursement are of great concern to both the buyer and seller. They are some of the greatest factors that influence both the price and probability that the practice will be sold. The potential purchaser will weigh whether the practice's existing payer mix and overall managed care strategy are as good as can be devised or whether a start-up practice could do equally well. The independent appraiser will be compelled to view the practice in the same way, which stresses the importance of positioning the practice with the best possible reimbursement scenario while blending this with the desire to treat a cross-section of patients.

The shift toward managed care has had the following influence on providers over the recent decades:

- They were forced to participate in large practice structures (ie, single specialty groups, multi-specialty groups, independent physician associations [IPAs]).
- They were forced to participate in integrated delivery systems (IDSs). Often, this entails the acquisition of physician practices by hospitals.
- They became employees for large insurance companies and/or HMOs.

An upheaval in the industry has resulted from these influences. Groups formed and hospitals bought up practices in an attempt to stay afloat in their marketplaces. Then, although many hospital practices have thrived and served their purpose well, others have been disengaged from hospitals or other integrated models due to mismanagement of competition that never materialized. At any rate, the industry is still in a state of flux; physicians still want to sell their practices, either for retirement or perhaps other financial or personal issues.

A practice's ability to engage in favorable managed care arrangements has a huge effect on the value of the practice. Patients are often represented by large employers, insurance organizations, and HMOs seeking to contract with providers who can offer seamless health care services. These services are designed to meet most medical needs within a single IDS. Providers with more integrated medical organizations are positioning themselves now and in the future by increasing their economic viability.

Whatever the motivation for optimizing the value, physicians respond to the pressures of managed care as they relate to the sale of the practice. The current movement toward increased managed care means different things to different providers (ie, primary care vs specialty care). An understanding of the implications of managed care to each of the provider groups is required to sufficiently address the question of valuation.

Primary Care Practices

In managed care, primary care physicians (eg, family practice, internal medicine, pediatrics, often obstetrics and gynecology) are case managers and, therefore, the patient's first point of access to health care services. Serving in the role of coordinators of care (or gatekeepers), primary care physicians are experiencing increased responsibility and significance in the industry.

Capitated plans place physicians at greater risk than traditional fee-for-service structures. Success or failure depends on the flow of patients through the system and referral decisions. Practice losses result from overutilization of provider services because fixed fees are not increased to cover additional services. Multi-specialty groups and integrated delivery systems are increasingly dependent upon primary care practitioners to efficiently direct patient flow through the system.

These factors contribute to why primary care physicians' practices are those most often acquired. Intangible assets of physicians play a pivotal role in the purchase price, particularly when considering the managed care gatekeeper function.

The influence of managed care must be considered when the independent appraiser values the primary care practice. When calculating the value of the intangible assets, particularly post-acquisition and what contribution this practice will make to the IDS and managed care environment in the area, the appraiser must weigh the following characteristics and issues:

- Operating reputations of the practice and number of years in practice in the service area
- Local health care scenes of managed care (ie, shifts from traditional payers to managed care and HMO penetration)
- Overall economic condition of the primary service area
- Practice's historical experience of providing service in a managed care environment
- Presence of several significant health care providers and/or payers (eg, competing hospitals, insurance companies, HMOs)
- General demographics of the practice (ie, heavily populated urban and suburban vs rural areas)

Primary care physicians are sought to serve on managed care panels and sources of referrals for local hospitals. Perceived as lower cost alternatives to specialists, they administer a larger portion of total health care service to defined patient populations. This advances the objectives of managed care, which is to provide medical services of quality at the lowest possible cost.

Specialty Care Practices

Primary care and the role of the primary care physician as a case manager poses specific issues for specialists. Most internal medicine specialists serve in multiple roles: personal physicians to local patients, consultants to other physicians, and co-managing patient care along with colleagues from other specialties or subspecialties. Many managed care organizations (MCOs), however, are inclined to force internists into a more limited role. Specialists in internal medicine are often given the opportunity to function as primary care physicians and coordinators of care, and internists who have subspecialized are being limited to the role of a consultant. Managed care accomplishes this through the contracting process, which may specifically limit internists to one role or the other by the way internists are listed in plan booklets provided to patients and in the referral mechanisms used to limit and control referrals from primary care physicians to consulting specialists.

Historically, specialists have been less pressured to control costs. Higher fees were tolerated due to medical need and expected as compensation for extended training. Compared with other providers, specialists have commanded a disproportionately higher portion of total health care spending. As cost containment pressures have mounted, managed care has placed emphasis on the primary care physician to regulate the use of specialists. Gatekeeper primary care physicians directly coordinate and authorize specialists (ie, consultant) referrals, diagnostic testing not provided in the primary care physician's office, and other ancillary services.

These limitations have caused controversy and difficulty for specialists. Some subspecialists in internal medicine, particularly those with subspecialties involving intense use of medical technology, are uncomfortable serving as primary care physicians and prefer to remain as consultants. However, as managed care systems limit referrals for this type of care, subspecialists may find an economic inducement to broaden their practice to include the primary care role. Other specialists in internal medicine without subspecialty training or practice may want to provide subspecialty services (for which they are qualified) to broaden the range of care that they can make available under a given managed care arrangement. This will increase the range of services they provide and increase earnings from fees from those services.

Because of managed care, specialists face a future of reduced fee-for-service arrangements, discounted pricing, and dependence upon primary care practitioners for referral revenues. Specialists are concerned, and understandably so, when one considers that such a significant portion of their economic livelihood is beyond their control.

Certain considerations for intangible assets must be made for valuation of both primary care and specialty practices. In addition, the following contribute significant value to the intangible assets of specialty practices:

- The reputation and prominence of the medical specialist
- The size of the medical specialty and its correlated market share within the service area
- The supply of medical providers in that specialty in the area vs the demands for services

This explanation shows the effect of managed care on both primary care and specialty practices and the value of practices. The increased emphasis on primary care physicians justifies a rise in the values of these practices (under certain market conditions). The appraiser of a primary care practice must consider these issues in compiling the information and calculating the value of the practice. For example, if it can be estimated that through current involvement and prospective growth in managed care, a practice's profitability will increase, a reflection of this in the valuation calculations will increase that practice's value. (See Chapter 3 for a review of methodologies of practice valuation, most of which depend upon expectations of increased earnings and cash flows to enhance value.)

Specialty practices are generally expected to experience a decline in value as managed care saturates health care. The ensuing fees and limited access to patients will drive down their margins, reducing their valuation amount.

Market dynamics in the geographical service area could justify premiums as significant intangible asset value. The relevance and appropriateness of any level of intangible asset value of a practice transfer may only be proven through extensive analysis and understanding of the operations of the practice, area market conditions, and competition.

The knowledge and experience of qualified and independent professional appraisers are essential to ensure accuracy in the valuation, particularly relating to managed care and IDSs.

Productivity Standards

After assessing the external issues, such as reimbursement through managed care and other third-party payers, the practice owner should also consider internal productivity standards. This relates essentially to the amount of work and volume of services by the individual providers. The question of how many patient encounters and procedures can or should be performed per individual provider is significant. Preparing for maximizing value would mean that the greater the individual productivity, the more likely the practice will carry a higher value. This is consistent with the methodologies that are applied to derive conclusions of fair market value.

A practice with providers who average only 5 to 10 encounters/ procedures per day versus the one that averages 10 to 15 (both statistics include surgical procedures) is more likely of lesser value.

The question the owner should ask in preparation for the sale of the practice is whether or not individual productivity can be increased. If so, then this should be used as a catalyst for improving productivity. In many instances, it may be a good idea to suspend the valuation and sale of the practice for a considerable period (eg, perhaps a year or more) to reach a level of consistent increased productivity.

The independent appraiser must also assess the productivity levels. If the appraiser cannot justifiably assume that the individual productivity will improve, then it must be assumed that productivity will either stay constant or perhaps decline, especially if there are indications of such. This will significantly affect the conclusions of value.

Whether productivity can be increased to enhance the value of the practice will depend upon the unique circumstances of each practice. Some physicians will say they simply cannot work harder or faster without compromising quality, which indeed may be the case.

Similarly, the appraiser will have to assess the realities of future productivity, although it may be impossible to consider what a new owner will produce. The appraiser's only option, therefore, is to base productivity assumptions upon the current provider's performance, both historically and prospectively.

Referral Patterns

Referral patterns also serve as a significant factor in levels of individual physician productivity. Primary care physicians must work with the marketplace directly, either through managed care arrangements or by other marketing initiatives to gain access to patients. Depending on the managed care environment, especially with HMOs where the primary care physician is the gatekeeper and must direct all referrals to specialists, the specialist must depend heavily on referrals. On the other hand, the practice specialty will determine whether the physician will be able to procure patients directly without any referrals. Even without the managed care factor, many patient referrals are from other physicians.

Strengthening the referral base is essential in maximizing the practice's value. For example, the appraiser must be convinced when valuing the practice that the historical referral base will be maintained, if not exceeded, under the new owner's direction. In this example, as with all cases, the first step is to make sure that the new owner will continue to garner the historical referrals, and that the referral stream will remain constant, particularly in a practice specialty that depends heavily upon referrals. The seller of the practice can be very effective in keeping referral patterns strong through good service, continual feedback, and responsiveness to other professionals. It is important to keep in mind, however, that financial incentives are prohibited and are not relevant in terms of maximizing practice value.[*]

Compensation Incentives

Another way to maintain productivity levels of the existing provider base in preparation for sale of the practice is through a well-planned and productivity-based compensation incentive model. An incentive plan model that is based upon productivity is usually responsive and used quite commonly among practices to improve their overall operating margins. It is also a strategy that can be used to improve productivity in preparation for maximizing value prior to a sale.

Compensation plans can be based on various measurements of productivity, including gross charges or full fee schedule charges, net charges, net collections, number of encounters, number of surgical procedures, number of new patients, and RVUs. Incentive programs used to motivate nonowner physicians to maximize productivity should always be equitable and lawful.

Provider Stability

Ensuring that revenue is maintained throughout the long term will largely depend upon the stability of the providers; however, it will also be the result of the strength of the support staff. Stability is the result of a good working environment; adequate support staff; training and education of providers and others staff members, as appropriate; a highly rewarded, productivity-based compensation plan; a reasonable reimbursement structure so there are enough monies to go around to pay the providers; and sound operational management.

---

[*] The Medicare Anti-Kickback Statute [Section 1128(b) of the Social Security Act, 42 U.S.C. § 1320a-7b(b)] prohibits knowingly and willingly soliciting, receiving, or offering any remuneration to induce referrals of items or services by any Medicare and state health care programs.

Practice stability is a key factor in maintaining the base of revenue, which is an outcome of having a successful referral base along with a high level of patient satisfaction.

ENHANCING VALUE THROUGH EXPENSE CONTROLS

Controls has 2 connotations in a medical practice. The first is controlling cost through careful management oversight. The second is more subtle and involves efficient operations, which inherently control expenses by supporting higher levels of productivity. An additional reason to initiate strong internal controls is to safeguard the practice's assets.

Controlling Operating Expenses

One way to increase value in the appraiser's eyes is to control operating expenses. Operating expenses can be divided into 2 major components: general overhead and provider cost. General overhead includes everyday clinical and nonclinical expenses of operation. Provider cost includes salaries, benefits, and expenses directly attributable to the physician and nonphysician providers.

In anticipation of bringing the medical practice to market and enhancing its value beforehand, the owner should review all major expense classifications, which generally consist of the following 4 major categories:

- Salaries and benefits
- Rent and other facility-related expenses
- Office and medical supply costs
- General and administrative expenses

The greatest single expense in the medical practice is salaries and benefits. To assess salary costs, the practice owner will need to review a list of all employees, their job descriptions, salaries, and associated benefits, in the same way the appraiser will examine them. Is the number of staff adequate? Will they fulfill their responsibilities in the best possible manner according to their job description?

Another consideration that is parallel to preparing the valuation is the employment of family members and their relative contribution. For example, some practices may employ family members that either draw a salary higher than market or do not function as an employee. The owner of the practice should review this from an appraiser's standpoint and make the appropriate payroll adjustments in preparation for the sale of the practice. Although all changes may not need to occur immediately, identifying these situations will enable the adjustments to be made prior to the transfer of ownership.

Job descriptions are also important in order to consider the individual credentials and resulting compensation. Long-term employees that have proven their value over time should be assured that every effort would be made to try to protect their position. Conversely, the practice may need to adjust for over- or under-qualified employees several years prior to the actual sale. By conducting a fair and objective analysis of the practice's staffing and job duties and notifying its employees of intentions to sell, the employer is being more than considerate.

Benefits are also a major consideration. While some benefit expenses may be adjusted under the new ownership (which the appraiser must denote), for the most part, the benefits that are established are those that would be expected by the employees under the new ownership. An exception might be retirement plans that are replaced with a less generous plan, at least at the commencement of the new ownership. Most other benefits could be expected to continue.

The objective in reviewing expenses prior to the valuation is to analyze every expense for its legitimacy and necessity, particularly salaries and benefits, which make up roughly half of the general overhead of most practices. Adjustments should be appropriately made not just to make the bottom line look good but also as a measure of proper planning. In the end, the new owner's perspective will be different, which should be imparted at the appropriate time to the staff. (This should not initiate an overreaction, nor should the staff be alarmed as a result of preparation to sell the practice.)

Evaluation of all other sources of administrative overhead should follow the consideration of personnel expense. Industry statistics and benchmarks should be used as a comparison as these are evaluated, preparing the practice for valuation and, ultimately, its sale. Adjustments should occur where warranted, taking care not to cut out necessary operational expenses, just the exorbitant ones.

This logic follows with each of the other major areas of general overhead, including rent and facility expenses, general administrative expenses, and supply purchases.

Rental rate and space may be difficult to adjust in the case of a long-term lease. The practice owner who is also the owner of the facility must decide whether to sell the real estate or lease it to the new owner. (The real estate is almost never a part of the practice review and valuation. It is and should be a separate legal entity subject to its own independent valuation.)

Thus, the rent should be considered in the context of who the owner/lessor shall be after the sale. For example, if the dermatologist owner of the practice is also the owner of the real estate, including the building, then a new lease can easily be consummated with the new owner of the practice. If there are other owners of the building, it is possible that a new lease may be negotiated or, at the very least, the existing lease assigned or sublet under the same terms and conditions of the existing lease. From a preplanning aspect, it depends on what the terms of the lease will be and who the lessor will be after the sale.

In ownership, there could be some flexibility in rental rate. Conversely, for the most part, everyone (no matter whom the lessor is) will want to obtain a market rental for the property. The current rent at market rates should be determined as an aspect of planning. For various internal reasons, the rent may be on the higher side of fair market value on some occasions (eg, when the dermatologist owner of the practice also owns the real estate). This may need to be adjusted in order to appeal to a new owner of the practice to lease the facilities, which is a matter to be considered by both the physician and the appraiser when preparing for the valuation. Rent believed to be significantly under or over market will be adjusted in the valuation calculations, particularly under the income approach (see Chapter 3).

In general, cost containment should be an overriding principle, whether the practice is ongoing or being prepared for valuation and subsequent sale. Figure 7-1 illustrates general overhead categories that should be considered and controlled prior to completion of the valuation.

Physician Compensation and Benefits

Perhaps the greatest expense is provider compensation and benefits. Compensation is simply a result of the monies left over after all other expenses are paid in practices where ownership is shared by the physicians and no providers are employees. Employed providers are usually paid using a combination of salary and incentive bonus. Planning for valuation and sale or merger calls for consideration of these historical compensation figures, as it is a major consideration within the valuation process. The independent appraiser must consider and render an opinion about the stability and viability of the provider base, which may include the current owners' knowledge of likely change in ownership, or their potential for exiting the practice, subject to the sale. If a prospective buyer sees the opportunity for market (or above-market) compensation after the acquisition, and this is substantiated in the valuation analysis, the prospects of sale increase immensely.

F I G U R E 7-1

General Overhead Categories

- Adequate number of personnel
- Appropriate compensation levels for personnel
- Health insurance and other benefits (ie, direct costs)
  - —Overtime
  - —Retirement plans
- Benefits (ie, indirect costs)
  - —Sick leave policy
  - —Bereavement pay
  - —Vacation
- Cost of medical supplies
- Cost of office supplies
- Leases and real estate
- Refunds to patients
- Rent (eg, leasing too much space)
- Advertising expense
- Professional fees, including fees for billing and collection services
- Utilities
- Postage and other shipping charges
- Telephone expenses
- Other smaller overhead items, such as bank service charges

Establishing Internal Controls

Another consideration of the practice owner prior to the valuation process and sale or merger is to ensure that sufficient internal controls are in place. Internal controls—important in every business—protect the practice from loss of income and potential employee theft. No measures totally prevent theft; however, having safeguards in place reduces exposure and risk to such losses.

In preparation for sale, the practice owner should see that internal controls are in place. Such controls include policies and procedures that document functions and separate duties, particularly for handling cash and other assets. Financial controls are provided in Figure 7-2.

A competent practice management operation should have well-documented and evenly enforced policies and procedures that safeguard the practice's assets. The independent appraiser of the practice will want assurance that these controls are in place. These protocols have a positive influence on the prospective buyer of the practice.

Enhancing Value Through Strategic Planning

Strategic planning—a commonly overused term—is often of minimal value to the practice. However, a successful plan for the future, considering organizing principles in key areas, is crucial both for the practice that is contemplating sale or merger and for continued operations under the same ownership.

A beneficial strategic plan considers organizing principles in the following 6 key areas:

1. Patients
2. Technical skills
3. Administrative skills
4. Support skills

FIGURE 7-2

Financial Controls

Separation of duties. Define job functions for practice staff to prevent one individual from having too much responsibility.

Reconciliation of payments with encounters and procedures. Establish a daily checks-and-balances routine.

Contractual adjustments. Confirm contractual adjustments. Payer mix can vary greatly. Without safeguards, an unethical employee could misstate adjustments and try to pocket the difference.

Systematic controls of forms, including a prenumbering system. All manual forms that have any relevance to financial data and information should be prenumbered and controlled.

Adherence to personnel policies and procedures, including mandatory time off. Require every employee to take at least a week of time off once per year (not as 1 or 2 days at a time where an unethical employee could cover for their fraud).

Accounts payable controls. Install proper protocols for the approval and payment of accounts payable.

5. Alliances

6. Subtractions (ie, areas of business that will not be sought out or accepted)

All businesses need a blueprint for action, or a strategic plan. Each will vary with the present issues of the organization. A medical practice contemplating sale or merger will differ significantly from one that plans to continue under current ownership for the foreseeable future. The important point is to have a plan for the future. First, a plan is necessary to achieve and maintain stability. Second, a strategic plan offers a significant advantage in the search for a partner or purchaser if the practice is to be sold or merged with another practice.

The busier the practice (ie, more services and locations, number of providers), the more useful the strategic plan. Long-term planning in key areas is important regardless of whether the practice is up for sale or in the throes of transition.

Several strategic questions/issues should be asked and considered when preparing the practice for sale or merger. They include the following:

- What is the nature of the practice and the services that are performed?

- How do regulatory forces influence its operations both now and in the future?

- Are there any significant services that will be changed due to the economy, regulatory matters, or other external issues?

- What effect does the future of electronic communications and data gathering have on the practice?

- What are some of the education standards and their effect on staffing (both clinical and nonclinical, provider and nonprovider)?

- What is the geographic range of the practice and where are the future opportunities or challenges relative to this?

- What emerging practices are in this area that would provide specific competition (eg, the presence of another dermatology or other specialty that does some similar procedures)?

- What capabilities does the practice have for meeting the demands of competition?

- Who are the key sources of patients (both primary and third-party payers)?

- How dependent is the practice on keeping these patients (likely represented by certain large payers)?

- Who are the key third-party payers in the practice's service area that are not served by the practice?

- What is the scope of clinical resources and challenges of the practice?

- Does the practice use information technology and specialized staff to leverage professional expertise?

- How are the practice's services marketed and to what extent should they be marketed?

- Who has responsibility for future development of the products and services within the practice?

Identification of strategic issues is a critical part of planning and is important, even if the practice is contemplating new ownership. To the potential new owner, a strategic plan ensures that the practice is an ongoing, viable, sustaining entity and helps the independent appraiser assess the practice's growth potential. It could even increase the value of the practice under the income approach through more aggressive, yet justified, growth projections.

Thus, setting a strategic plan for the practice in preparation for sale or merger is important. Strategic planning sets out the following major areas:

- Identifying the practice's capabilities
- Determining future opportunities
- Establishing goals
- Establishing priorities
- Developing a clear plan to realize the results desired for the future

Part of the strategic plan may be the sale or merger of the practice, which is not necessarily a negative in the context of the overall process under consideration. In fact, most prospective buyers should be impressed by the fact that the existing owners have thought through their situation enough to conclude possible sale or merger as a part of their ongoing strategic initiatives.

Other basic considerations and questions in strategic planning include:

- Who are we?
- Where are we today?
- How do we want to conduct ourselves?
- Where are we going?
- How are we going to get to where we want to go?
- What is the best way to measure our progress?
- Do we need a major change in ownership to effectuate our goals and objectives?

Additionally, it is also good for the practice to define its mission and values, typically through statements that are periodically updated to clarify the practice's vision for the future.

An environmental assessment that reviews the widest range of factors that influence the practice's operations and breaks them down into various concerns for the future should follow. This could include economic, social, technological, regulatory, and political forces that affect the profession.

Usually, the environmental assessment calls for a strengths, weaknesses, opportunities, and threats (SWOT) analysis as an important part of the inward review of the practice and consideration of its strategic issues. The SWOT analysis should include a frank look at the providers and the services that are delivered by those individuals and be objective and practical in nature, realizing that there are limitations to the practice's performance results.

Thus, the practice should be thoroughly prepared for a dramatic change in the future (eg, any change in ownership) through effective strategic planning and direction. Otherwise, it is less likely to sell, and the independent appraiser's understanding of the practice's plans for the future is compromised.

Personnel Policies and Procedures Manual

Value is maximized by having sound personnel policies in place. Every practice should have a personnel policy and procedure manual. This is a simple booklet stating policies, benefits, and other protocols. Such resources, although subjective, say a lot about the management of the practice. While the appraiser will not place great emphasis in this area when deriving value, having access to the policy book that establishes the operations of the practice may positively affect the valuation to some degree.

CONCLUSION

The focus of this chapter has been on the components that must be considered when selling a practice. These components show how value can be enhanced through a number of operational initiatives. The valuation process must review each of these facets within the operations of the practice and relate them to the calculations. It must also conduct a subjective overview of the work being completed to derive, in the opinion of the appraiser, the fair market value of the medical practice. If the practice is strong and is instituting sound operational systems, the practice will have greater value in the eyes of a potential purchaser.

South Atlanta Orthopedic and Physical Therapy, Inc

Appendix A provides an example of valuation operating results of a fictional practice: South Atlanta Orthopedic and Physical Therapy, Inc. These hypothetical financial statements reveal where an appraiser may gather information in a real appraisal.

The figures used in this example are not from any actual medical practice. Names have not been changed. *This is a fictional example.* Any similarity to any medical practice or otherwise is completely happenstance. However, the numbers that have been used are close to what a physician practice with a physical therapy component would resemble.

This book is not meant to be a "mini MBA." It does not delve into the volumes of information about appraisals and appraisal theory, and it is not directed toward people with a PhD. It is meant for individuals that have a general understanding of financial management, accounting, and finance. The financial examples have been laid out accordingly.

OVERVIEW OF THE PRACTICE

South Atlanta Orthopedic and Physical Therapy, Inc, is a 2-physician orthopedic practice that specializes in sports medicine. In addition to the orthopedic services that it provides, it also offers an in-house physical therapy suite with a full range of free weights, body building equipment, cardiovascular equipment, a therapeutic pool, and other exercise equipment. In addition to the physician-providers, there are 2 full-time physical therapists that work in the physical therapy center. Table A-1 provides the staff breakdown.

The practice owns a considerable amount of physical therapy and medical equipment (which includes an x-ray machine); however, it does not own its own facility. This space is leased, and the rent is assumed to be fair market value for the area. The practice has operated in its current capacity for approximately 9 years, and while it has offered the same services for this period, it has recently upgraded some of its equipment and invested in some more technologically advanced physical therapy equipment. The practice has had stable operations over its history. Both of the physicians are somewhat entrenched in the community and are expected to remain on as employees of the larger group. The practice has financed most of its growth in purchasing

TABLE A-1

Staff Information

Position	FTE	Individual Compensation*	Total Compensation
Physical therapist	2	$50,000	$100,000
Office manager	1	$38,000	$38,000
PSR	2	$23,000	$46,000
Billing	1	$30,000	$30,000
RN/x-ray	2	$33,000	$66,000
Medical assistant	1.25	$28,000	$35,000
Total Staff	**9**		**$315,000**

*Approximate compensation

equipment through the acquisition of debt; however, it presently has an excellent credit rating through its lenders.

Currently, Atlanta Orthopedic Physicians, PA, (AOP) are considering the purchase of a 100% interest in the practice, as defined in the sample letter of agreement in Chapter 2. AOP is a large orthopedic group consisting of more than 275 orthopedic physicians (not including nonphysician providers). In addition to orthopedic services, AOP provides physical therapy and a host of other ancillary services (including imaging, lab, etc). AOP's operations are centered in Atlanta, Georgia, but it provides services all over the southeastern United States with practices in Louisiana, Mississippi, Alabama, Georgia, Tennessee, South Carolina, and North Carolina.

The effective date of this valuation is as of January 1, 2004.

FINANCIAL STATEMENTS FOR SOUTH ATLANTA ORTHOPEDIC AND PHYSICAL THERAPY, INC

Tables A-2 through A-5 and Figure A-1 provide the financial information of the practice that forms the basis for the valuation.

MARKET ANALYSIS DATA

The resources used to obtain data for this analysis are from 2 sources: publicly traded market data and previously acquired company data. Each of these resource categories denotes the companies used to obtain data and describes how they relate to the entity at hand.

Publicly Traded Market Data

The following companies were used when completing the guideline publicly traded company method. The companies are all publicly traded companies. (Stock tickers are provided in parenthesis.) A brief description of the company and what it does follows.

National Physical Therapy (NPT)

NPT provides physical therapy services in 35 states across the United States and in Mexico and Canada. It does not employ any

TABLE A-2

Income Statement for Last 4 Years

South Atlanta Orthopedics and Physical Therapy, LLC
Profit and Loss Statement for the Fiscal Year January 1 through December 31

	FY 2003	Percent to Net Revenue	FY 2002	Percent to Net Revenue	FY 2001	Percent to Net Revenue	FY 2000	Percent to Net Revenue
Revenue								
Fees from medical operations	$3,689,023	156.25%	$3,347,571	161.29%	$3,218,818.06	163.93%	$3,008,241.18	161.29%
Less discounts and reimbursements	($1,328,048)	-56.25%	($1,272,077)	-61.29%	($1,255,339.04)	-63.93%	($1,143,131.65)	-61.29%
Net Revenue	*$2,360,975*	100.00%	*$2,075,494*	100.00%	*$1,963,479*	100.00%	*$1,865,110*	100.00%
Expenses								
Personnel Expenses								
Physician benefits	$155,656	6.59%	$148,244	7.14%	$141,185	7.19%	$133,193	7.14%
Physician compensation	$695,125	29.44%	$662,024	31.90%	$630,499	32.11%	$594,810	31.89%
Staff benefits	$75,025	3.18%	$71,452	3.44%	$68,050	3.47%	$64,198	3.44%
Staff salary	$315,151	13.35%	$300,144	14.46%	$285,851	14.56%	$269,671	14.46%
Total personnel expenses	*$1,240,957*	52.56%	*$1,181,864*	56.94%	*$1,125,585*	54.23%	*$1,061,872*	51.16%
G&A expenses								
Advertising and promotion	$35,252	1.49%	$32,337	1.56%	$35,152	1.79%	$30,362	1.63%
Amortization	$14,500	0.61%	$14,500	0.70%	$8,561	0.44%	$7,321	0.39%
Automotive	$15,325	0.65%	$13,352	0.64%	$10,520	0.54%	$8,525	0.46%
CME	$4,985	0.21%	$3,352	0.16%	$3,362	0.17%	$3,299	0.18%

Continued

TABLE A-2

Income Statement for Last 4 Years—*Continued*

South Atlanta Orthopedics and Physical Therapy, LLC
Profit and Loss Statement for the Fiscal Year January 1 through December 31

	FY 2003	Percent to Net Revenue	FY 2002	Percent to Net Revenue	2001	Percent to Net Revenue	2000	Percent to Net Revenue
Depreciation	$75,895	3.21%	$50,325	2.42%	$45,935	2.34%	$50,436	2.70%
Dues and subscriptions	$4,567	0.19%	$4,012	0.19%	$40,012	2.04%	$38,765	2.08%
Insurance	$55,011	2.33%	$57,023	2.75%	$55,252	2.81%	$54,358	2.91%
Interest expense	$75,898	3.21%	$55,025	2.65%	$50,253	2.56%	$50,253	2.69%
Laundry	$1,255	0.05%	$2,025	0.10%	$2,033	0.10%	$2,145	0.12%
Leased equipment	$4,035	0.17%	$4,035	0.19%	$6,736	0.34%	$6,735	0.36%
Outside services	$4,585	0.19%	$3,385	0.16%	$22,265	1.13%	$1,657	0.09%
Payroll expense	$8,211	0.35%	$8,025	0.39%	$7,598	0.39%	$7,435	0.40%
Professional fees	$85,426	3.62%	$34,554	1.66%	$35,425	1.80%	$33,452	1.79%
Professional liability	$155,252	6.58%	$98,058	4.72%	$97,025	4.94%	$96,025	5.15%
Rental expense	$135,000	5.72%	$128,571	6.19%	$122,449	6.24%	$116,618	6.25%
Supplies: computer	$5,688	0.24%	$4,658	0.22%	$3,555	0.18%	$3,758	0.20%
Supplies: laboratory	$80,122	3.39%	$78,025	3.76%	$77,001	3.92%	$76,050	4.08%
Supplies: medical	$135,002	5.72%	$122,589	5.91%	$120,569	6.14%	$119,985	6.43%
Supplies: office	$20,133	0.85%	$19,857	0.96%	$19,235	0.98%	$19,777	1.06%
Travel and entertainment	$7,022	0.30%	$5,552	0.27%	$5,032	0.26%	$4,998	0.27%
Utilities	$52,023	2.20%	$54,023	2.60%	$53,252	2.71%	$52,025	2.79%
Total G&A expenses	*$975,187*	41.30%	*$793,283*	38.22%	*$821,222*	41.82%	*$783,979*	42.03%
Total expenses	*$2,216,144*	93.87%	*$1,975,147*	95.17%	*$1,946,807*	99.15%	*$1,845,851*	98.97%
Net income before taxes	***$144,831***	6.13%	***$100,347***	4.83%	***$16,672***	0.85%	***$19,258***	1.03%

Balance Sheet for Last 4 Years

	South Atlanta Orthopedics and Physical Therapy, LLC Balance Sheet			
	FY 2003	**FY 2002**	**FY 2001**	**FY 2000**
Assets				
Current assets				
Cash (money market account)	$12,502	$14,300	$10,050	$9,580
Accounts receivable	$225,898	$200,123	$215,023	$203,323
Total current assets	*$238,400*	*$214,423*	*$225,073*	*$212,903*
Long-term assets				
Property, plant, & equipment	$753,252	$717,383	$650,130	$663,261
Accumulated depreciation	$102,589	$85,012	$93,946	$90,333
Total long-term assets	*$650,663*	*$632,371*	*$556,184*	*$572,928*
Total Assets	**$889,063**	**$846,794**	**$781,257**	**$785,831**

Liabilities				
Current liabilities				
Accounts payable	$5,252	$5,252	$4,235	$5,674
Short-term debt	$15,250	$20,120	$14,757	$13,654
Total current liabilities	*$20,502*	*$25,372*	*$18,992*	*$19,328*
Long-term liabilities				
Long-term debt				
Eastern Bank loan	$455,005	$470,132	$454,021	$458,923
Central Bank line of credit	$55,121	$12,525	$0	$0
Total long-term liabilities	*$510,126*	*$482,657*	*$454,021*	*$458,923*
Total liabilities	*$530,628*	*$508,029*	*$473,013*	*$478,251*
Equity	*$337,933*	*$313,393*	*$289,252*	*$288,252*
Total Liabilities and Equity	**$889,063**	**$846,794**	**$781,257**	**$785,831**

physicians. The majority of NPT's locations are in the eastern, mid-Atlantic states and the Midwest. It does not have a presence in the western United States.

Physical Therapy Associates (PTA)

PTA provides physical therapy services in 10 states, mostly in the southwest to mid-southern states. It is focused on rural areas and cities with populations of 50,000 or less. It owns very little real estate in which it occupies and it does not employ its physicians, but it does employ all other providers (eg, physical therapists).

Orthopedics of America (OA)

OA is an orthopedic medical practice management company. It is based out of the Northwest and the majority of its services are

TABLE A-4

Adjusted Expenses

	FY 2003	FY 2002	FY 2001	FY 2000	Average
Actual Expenses	**$2,216,144**	**$1,975,147**	**$1,946,807**	**$1,845,851**	**$1,995,987**
Expense Adjustments					
Backed-out					
Physician benefits	($155,656)	($148,244)	($141,185)	($133,193)	**($144,569)**
Physician compensation	($695,125)	($662,024)	($630,499)	($594,810)	**($645,614)**
Amortization	($14,500)	($14,500)	($8,561)	($7,321)	**($11,221)**
Automotive	($15,325)	($13,352)	($10,520)	($8,525)	**($11,931)**
CME	($4,985)	($3,352)	($3,362)	($3,299)	**($3,750)**
Depreciation	($75,895)	($50,325)	($45,935)	($50,436)	**($55,648)**
Outside services	$0	$0	($22,265)	$0	**($5,566)**
Professional fees	($85,426)	$0	$0	$0	**($21,357)**
Travel and entertainment	($7,022)	($5,552)	($5,032)	($4,998)	**($5,651)**
Total backed-out expenses	*($1,053,934)*	*($897,349)*	*($867,358)*	*($802,582)*	**($905,306)**
Added expenses					
Physician benefits	$141,674	$137,547	$133,541	$129,651	**$135,603**
Physician compensation	$708,368	$687,736	$667,705	$648,257	**$678,016**
Outside services	$0	$0	$2,500	$0	**$625**
Professional services	$35,000	$0	$0	$0	**$8,750**
Total expenses added	*$885,042*	*$825,283*	*$803,746*	*$777,908*	**$822,995**
Total expense adjustments	*($168,892)*	*($72,066)*	*($63,613)*	*($24,674)*	**($82,311)**
Adjusted Expenses	**$2,047,252**	**$1,903,082**	**$1,883,194**	**$1,821,178**	**$1,913,676**

provided to practices in Washington, Oregon, Idaho, Montana, and Canada (though, it does have a minimal presence in California). It does not own any real estate associated with its operations. Its primary line of business is associated with providing management services to smaller orthopedic practices (1-5 physicians). The services that OA provides range from employing the staff to billing and collections. Services are provided via a contract.

National Ortho (NO)

NO is a nationwide provider of orthopedic and allied care services ranging from physical therapy to podiatry and surgical care services. NO is located in all 50 states and in Puerto Rico, Europe, Mexico, and Canada. Locations consist of full-service sites that provide "1-stop" physician and ancillary services and sites that just provide one service or another (ie, surgical center only, physical therapy center only, etc). A major entrance into the western US market was made in 2001 with the purchase of StrengthPac, a provider of physical therapy services. NO owns approximately half of its real estate through a subsidiary venture, Healthcare Facility Managers, Inc. (This information is not included on its financial statements.)

TABLE A-5

Balance Sheet Adjustments

	FY 2003 Balance Sheet	Adjustments	FY 2003 Balance Sheet Adjusted
Assets			
Current assets			
Cash (money market account)	$12,502	$0	$12,502
Accounts receivable *	$225,898	($75,898)	$150,000
Total current assets	*$238,400*	*($75,898)*	*$162,502*
Long-term assets			
Property, plant, & equipment	$753,252	($75,325)	$677,927
Accumulated depreciation	$102,589	$0	$0
Total long-term assets	*$650,663*	*($75,325)*	*$677,927*
Total Assets	**$889,063**		**$840,429**

	FY 2003 Balance Sheet	Adjustments	FY 2003 Balance Sheet Adjusted
Liabilities			
Current liabilities			
Accounts payable	$5,252	$0	$5,252
Short-term debt	$15,250	$0	$15,250
Total current liabilities	*$20,502*	*$0*	*$20,502*
Long-term liabilities			
Long-term debt			
Eastern Bank loan	$372,609	$0	$372,609
Central Bank line of credit	$55,121	$0	$55,121
Total long-term liabilities	*$427,730*	*$0*	*$427,730*
Total liabilities	*$448,232*	*$0*	*$448,232*
Equity	*$420,329*	*$0*	*$420,329*
Total Liabilities and Equity	**$889,063**	**$0**	**$889,063**

*Discounted to fair collectible value.

†Discount based on in-place value of furniture and equipment.

Northern Health Associates (NHA)

NHA provides orthopedic management and physical therapy services in Illinois, Indiana, Ohio, and Kentucky. This company is fairly new, having only operated since 2001.

Table A-6 and Figure A-2 summarize the guideline public companies' operations.

Previously Acquired Company Data

The following comparables of recent transactions were used to complete the market approach.

FIGURE A-1

Performance Summary for Last 4 Years

	FY 2003	FY 2002	FY 2001	FY 2000	Average
Revenue	$2,360,975	$2,075,494	$1,963,479	$1,865,110	$1,968,027
Expenses	$2,216,144	$1,975,147	$1,946,807	$1,845,851	$1,922,602
Percent to total	93.87%	95.17%	99.15%	98.97%	**97.69%**
Profit	$144,831	$100,347	$16,672	$19,258	**$45,426**
Adjusted expenses	$2,047,252	$1,903,082	$1,883,194	$1,821,178	$1,869,151
Percent to total	86.71%	91.69%	95.91%	97.64%	**94.98%**
Adjusted profit	$313,723	$172,412	$80,285	$43,932	**$98,876**

Revenue to expense correlation	0.9390
Revenue to adjusted expense correlation	0.9473

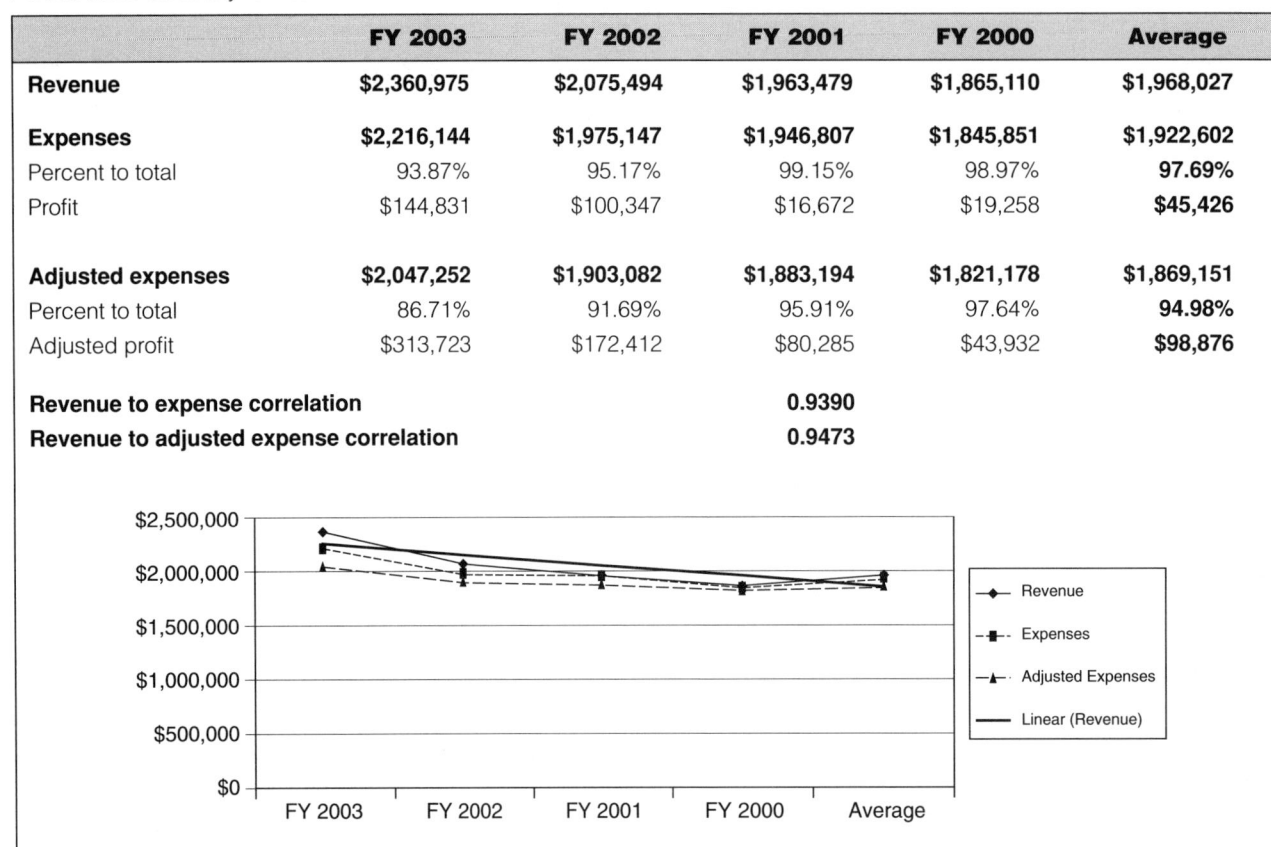

TABLE A-6

Guideline Public Company Data

Public Company	As Of	Price Per Share	Revenue	EBITDA	Shares Outstanding	Market Capitalization	Invested Capital
NPT	12/31/2003	$22.75	$102,325,455	$19,568,467	100,555,232	$2,287,631,528.00	$105,858,632
PTA	12/31/2003	$7.58	$77,258,952	$7,035,111	13,585,653	$102,979,249.74	$102,589,325
OA	12/31/2003	$9.81	$45,895,235	$8,987,025	15,252,222	$149,624,297.82	$32,577,789
NO	4/30/2003	$32.55	$195,556,216	$37,632,141	55,200,011	$1,796,760,358.05	$232,527,002
NHA	12/31/2003	$1.03	$39,958,567	$5,552,325	7,000,111	$7,210,114.33	$45,656,578
High		$32.55	$195,556,216	$37,632,141	100,555,232	$2,287,631,528	$232,527,002
Low		$1.03	$39,958,567	$5,552,325	7,000,111	$7,210,114	$32,577,789
Average		$14.74	$92,198,885	$15,755,014	38,318,646	$868,841,110	$103,841,865

Orthopedics Associates of Kentucky (OAK)

OAK provided orthopedic management services to orthopedic practices throughout Kentucky and Ohio. It provided services to approximately 25 different practices ranging in size of 1 to 5 physicians. The 100% purchase of OAK was made by NHA in June 2001 and consisted of a stock and debt transaction.

FIGURE A-2

Graphical Representation of Stock Prices

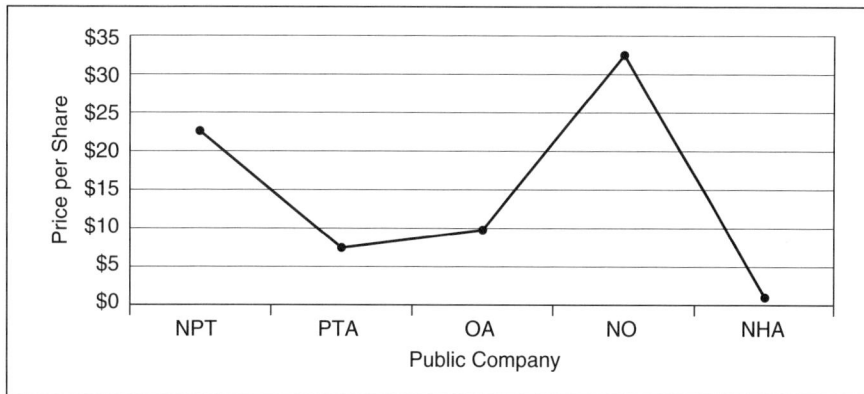

National Orthopedic Consultants (NOC)
NOC provided a wide range of orthopedic and physical therapy services across the Midwest. At the time of its purchase, NOC employed approximately 42 full-time providers at more than 15 locations. A 100% interest of NOC was purchased by NO in September 2002.

Physical Therapy Services of California (PTSC)
PTSC provided physical therapy services in and around the Sacramento, California, vicinity. It was purchased in 1996 by California-based StrengthPac, Inc, in order to expand its services into the northern California area.

Rehabilitative Associates of New Orleans (RAN)
RAN had 2 locations in the greater-New Orleans area. A 100% interest was purchased in early 2003, which included a pure equity purchase. The acquirer was Southern Rehab (SORB) of Dallas, Texas.

StrengthPac (SP)
SP provided physical therapy services in the western half of the United States with the majority of its clinics in California, Arizona, Nevada, and Colorado. It was purchased by NO to expand its services into the western United States.

Health Source (HS)
HS managed a number of orthopedic practices in the eastern United States, ranging from New York to Florida. At its peak in the 1990s, HS managed more than 390 practices; however, this figure had decreased considerably by the time it was acquired by American Physician Managers (AMPM). The acquisition was made in 2002 for 100% equity interest.

Table A-7 summarizes the information from these transactions.

In order to determine if the time in which the transaction occurred has any bearing on the price that was paid, a regression analysis was run comparing the date of the transaction to the transaction price and the transaction multiple (see Figure A-3). Based on the analysis,

TABLE A-7

Previous Transactional Information

Target	Date	Revenue	Net Income	Total Assets	Invested Capital	Transaction Price	Price to Revenue	Price to Income	Price to Assets	Price to Invested Capital
PTSC	07/01/96	$9,585,235	$53,252	$6,252,535	$5,663,210	$22,523,852	2.3498487	422.9672501	3.602355205	3.977223518
SP	04/01/01	$95,251,325	$3,258,958	$29,024,361	$28,974,069	$89,593,262	0.94059859	27.49138283	3.086829784	3.092187777
OAK	06/01/01	$5,253,250	$111,235	$334,558	$279,090	$7,532,892	1.433948889	67.72051962	22.51595239	26.99090616
HS	05/01/02	$33,589,257	$989,585	$19,992,536	$19,892,284	$35,896,552	1.068691457	36.27434935	1.79549768	1.804546527
NOC	09/01/02	$25,869,252	$979,798	$55,252	$54,227	$32,589,027	1.259759153	33.26096502	589.8252914	600.9741826
RAN	01/01/03	$2,358,952	($225,896)	$746,212	$672,691	$852,325	0.361315109	–3.773085845	1.142202216	1.267037912
High		$95,251,325	$3,258,958	$29,024,361	$28,974,069	$89,593,262	2.35	422.97	589.83	600.97
Low		$2,358,952	($225,896)	$55,252	$54,227	$852,325	0.36	(3.77)	1.14	1.27
Average		$28,651,212	$861,155	$9,400,909	$9,255,929	$31,497,985	1.24	97.32	103.66	106.35
SAOPT		$2,360,975	$144,831	$889,063	$848,059	$0				

FIGURE A-3

Transaction Price and Transaction Multiple Compared to Date of Transaction

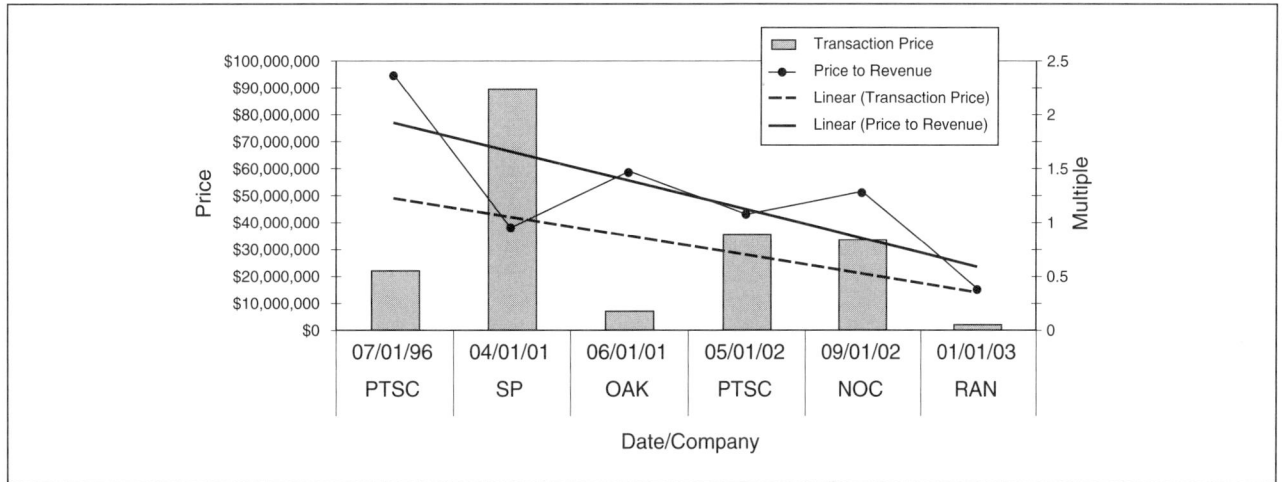

it would appear that both the amount and the multiple paid for these entities has decreased over time. To make this conclusion, however, additional research would have to be included. (Because this includes a number of different types of entities, this data may have to be adjusted.)

Informational Sites and World Wide Web Research

There are literally thousands of sites providing information on general appraisal topics as well as health care appraisal topics. This appendix provides a number of the more useful sites. Some of these sites are free (but often plagued with pop-up adds); some are a combination of free and pay sites; and some are outright pay sites. It can cost a small fortune to subscribe to every pay site, so it is best to make use of the free sites (and deal with the pop-ups) and be more discriminating when choosing pay sites. Also, a number of sites that may prove to be invaluable to appraisers are included in this appendix.

GENERAL SEARCH ENGINES

Various items can be found by using general search engines. They serve as a good way to begin any search. A few engines are meta-searches that compile searches of smaller engines or sort unrelated material and return only the most pertinent information from each search. A good rule of thumb is to search in more than one engine to get a comprehensive listing on the Internet.

www.google.com
Google is a great search engine and widely used for business searches.

www.lycos.com
Lycos will return a comprehensive search of related sites and information.

www.search.msn.com

www.hotbot.com
Hotbot is a meta-search engine that filters nonrelated subjects from smaller engine searches and displays only the most pertinent ones.

www.go.com or www.infoseek.com
This search engine is much like Yahoo. It is powered by Google for searching the Web.

www.yahoo.com
Yahoo is a commonly used search engine.

www.metacrawler.com
Metacrawler compiles several search engines and sorts each search into categories.

www.dogpile.com
Dogpile uses several smaller engines and filters nonrelated material to provide only the most useful information from each search.

www.askjeeves.com
With Ask Jeeves, the user types in a question and Ask Jeeves returns Web sites that can answer the question.

www.search.com
This engine will compile searchable databases from many different sources on the Web.

www.business.com
This Web site will compile hundreds of company Web sites and provide related links to more companies with similar functions.

www.findarticles.com
This database of articles can give insight into almost any search as well as provide links to related material.

www.highway61.com
This search engine uses the likes of Yahoo, Excite, Lycos, WebCrawler, and Infoseek to create a search engine with an attitude.

NEWS AND BUSINESS SOURCES

It is imperative that the appraiser be well-informed as to what is going on in the marketplace, especially when performing valuations. The following sites are some news sources for general business. This list is broad and may not contain every possible site, but it will provide the health care appraiser with a wealth of market information.

www.wsj.com
A business news periodical, the *Wall Street Journal* has nonmember and member information.

www.economist.com
This is an online journal providing daily information for business and economic occurrences.

www.ceoexpress.com
CEO Express is an excellent resource providing comprehensive information about and links to US and world news.

www.cnbc.com
This is the CNBC Web site.

www.bloomberg.com
Bloomberg provides current financial news.

www.cnnfn.com
CNN financial news is a link from CNN.com.

www.cfo.com
This is the link to the CFO magazine.

www.hoovers.com
This is a member Web site that allows users to research any type of information on thousands of publicly traded companies.

www.djinteractive.com
The Dow Jones interactive member site has reports and historical information on companies that comprise the Dow Jones Industrial Averages.

http://majournal.nvst.com/
This is the *Mergers and Acquisitions Journal* online site. This member site allows users to peruse useful archival information from the journal.

www.biz.yahoo.com/news
This Yahoo site can provide quick and easily accessible information to most publicly traded companies.

www.foxnews.com
Fox News offers fair and balanced reporting.

www.nytimes.com
This is the *The New York Times* Web site.

www.usatoday.com
This is the link to *USA Today.*

www.dismal.com
This is an economics site that uses government statistics to provide economic profiles, both as historical and forecasted, for different areas of the United States.

www.rollcall.com
This biweekly journal is considered a must read for insiders in Congress.

www.hillnews.com
This is a useful journal for those looking to stay current on the happenings on Capitol Hill.

www.compustat.com
Standard & Poor's COMPUSTAT databases is a leading resource for in-depth financial information on publicly traded companies in the United States and around the world.

HEALTH CARE INFORMATION AND NEWS SITES

As well as being current on general news, anyone valuing a medical practice must know current information and where to find it, including archival press releases and articles pertaining to various sectors of the industry. The following sites are excellent resources.

www.mpmnetwork.com
This is the link to the *Medical Practice Management and Healthcare Office Management Magazine* for administrators.

www.uoworks.com
Unique Opportunities provides resources for physicians including recruiting resources.

www.webmd.com
WebMD keeps visitors updated on current and recent health issues.

www.medicaleconomics.com
This link provides current news and financial information from the *Medical Economics* magazine.

www.msnbc.com/healthlibrary
This daily health news site also lets visitors search archival information.

www.bcbshealthissues.com
At the Blue Cross Blue Shield Web site, visitors can search for information on health-related issues and conditions.

www.forbes.com/healthcare
Daily news is provided to members of the *Forbes Magazine* online.

www.nih.gov/news/
This site from the National Institute of Health provides recent press releases in the world of medicine.

www.reutershealth.com
This membership Web site provides current information on health-related issues.

www.worldhealthnews.harvard.edu
This is a weekly journal from the Harvard School of Public Health.

www.medscape.com
This search engine, courtesy of Web MD, provides articles covering most, if not all, health-related questions.

www.healthleaders.com
Visitors can access updates, press releases, and archival searches from the health magazine.

HEALTH CARE SITES AND ASSOCIATIONS

Many sites on the Internet can give appraisers and researchers valuable information on new advances in medical specialties. They provide links to a wealth of current trends and news for hospitals and clinical physicians alike. Following is a short list of organizations that can serve as a springboard to anyone interested in finding specific information on different health care specialties.

www.cancer.org
The National Cancer Society has links and information about cancer and support groups for families.

www.mayoclinic.com
The Mayo Clinic site has information and links for health conditions and questions.

www.hospitalconnect.com
This is the American Hospital Association Web site that allows free membership. Users can peruse and find information and links to several different areas.

www.ncqa.org
This is the National Commission on Quality Assurance site that can provide information on current issues as well as links to related sites.

www.ahca.org
The American Health Care Association provides information links and research about handicapped and elderly people.

www.ichp.edu
This site offers links, research, and other information pertaining to child health care programs.

www.leapfrog.com
The Leapfrog Group has put together statistics about health procedures in hospitals, success rates, etc. This Web site is interesting for patients or researchers looking at hospitals.

www.healthatoz.com
This Web site is geared toward the consumer and families. It is easy to navigate and provides links to other such Web sites.

www.asco.org
This is the American Society of Clinical Oncology Web site. This free membership Web site provides great information about different cancers and links to more information.

www.americanheart.org
The American Heart Association will help anyone who has questions about the heart and provides access to a myriad of links on the subject.

www.rsna.org
The Radiologist Society of North America is a solid site for radiologists.

www.naph.org
At the National Association of Public Hospital and Health Systems, the researcher can gain links to various other associations and organizations pertaining to health.

http://www.physicianswebsites.com/healthcare-links.htm
This is a site dedicated to providing links to various medical professions and resources, including links to managed care sites and coding Web sites.

GOVERNMENT SITES

Not to be overlooked, government Web sites can also provide much helpful information on all types of issues. They can provide general information, including statistics, and specific information about regulations that govern the administration and organization of health care as well as general business information that appraisers should consider when evaluating companies.

www.infoctr.edu/fwl/
This Web site compiles overviews of industries that are regulated by the national government.

www.cdc.gov
Visitors can find information and statistics on various diseases and health conditions.

www.os.dhhs.gov
This is the Department of Health and Human Resources Web site.

Visitors can find information on a plethora of health-related conditions and recent developments in the industry.

www.nih.gov
The National Institute of Health can be a good springboard for further research.

www.nlm.nih.gov
This is the National Library of Medicine Web site.

www.fedstats.gov
When looking for statistical information from the federal government, this is a good place to start.

www.firstgov.gov
This site is a starting point for searching different government Web sites.

www.sec.gov
This is the Securities and Exchange Commission's Web site. It is good for researchers who want to stay current on market regulations.

http://cms.hhs.gov
This is the site for Medicare and Medicaid Services. It gives information on subjects relating to Medicare and Medicaid issues and initiatives.

http://www.nursingnetwork.com/webgov.htm
This site focuses on nursing links but has links to many different health care sites including the World Health Organization.

VALUATION RESOURCES

Many World Wide Web sites provide great resources for those who seek to value or appraise companies. Often times an appraiser must gather market data along with data from past mergers and acquisitions. These sites can provide data and starting places of searches for comparative analysis and information. Sometimes these sites charge a fee for their service; however, the fees are worth the cost for anyone looking to accurately appraise the value of a business.

www.valuationresources.com
This site has any information that may be needed and provides links to resources that contain general business information.

www.bvmarketdata.com
This site contains great information and links to mergers and acquisitions and related materials useful to business appraisers.

www.bizminer.com
This site provides financial analysis and market data on thousands of companies, including hard-to-find industry analysis.

www.levinassociates.com
For a fee, the user can find information including mergers and acquisitions and financial analysis.

www.marketresearch.com
This site offers information on current publicly traded stocks and financial analysis of a multitude of companies.

www.bvlibrary.com
This Web site is a solid guide and provides links for those interested in valuations and appraisals.

www.appraisalfoundation.org
This site is a good starting point for appraisers who are looking for the standard in the business. It is a nonprofit organization aimed at creating uniform techniques and strategies for business appraisers.

www.financialweb.com/market
This site is helpful when comparing stock prices for more than one day at a time. Archival information on historical prices as well as other market data is available.

www.djindexes.com
This Web site from the Dow Jones Industrial can be a basis for beginning a business search.

www.multexinvestor.com
This is another Web site that pulls together information about mergers and acquisitions, financial forecasts, and historical data about publicly traded companies.

www.xls.com
This site allows users to download financial information on tons of companies. Material is already in the form of Microsoft spreadsheets.

www.ibbotson.com
This site provides an industry-leading lineup of asset allocation products and services.

A

Amortization   The recovery of an expense item over a period based upon the economic value and life of the *asset*.

Appraisal and Valuation   The term *appraisal* has been referred to as the overall process of review, while a *valuation* is the actual determination of monetary worth. Within the context of physician practice reviews, the terms are synonymous.

Asset-based Approach   Estimating the reproduction costs of assets of the practice. *Tangible* and *intangible assets* are valued individually on a going-concern basis, then accumulated to derive total value.

Assets   The economic resources of the practice (ie, property and equipment, cash and accounts receivable).

B

Book Value   *Asset* cost minus *liability*. This is generally an accounting term that reflects an owner's *equity*.

Business Enterprise Value   The combination of net working *capital*, fixed *assets*, and *intangible assets*.

C

Capital   Money accumulated for investment or retirement purposes.

Capitalization   A process of converting net income that results from period-to-period operations into a lump sum present value. Rates for such capitalization are normally called *CAP rates*.

Capitalization of Earnings   Earnings, whether average or weighted, times a multiplier or divisor factor. Excess earnings equal income that is attributable to goodwill.

Capitalization Rate   Standard of measurement (either multiplied or divided) used to measure present or investment value in monetary terms. Generally calculated as the *discount rate* less long-term growth ($r_e - g$).

Capitation   A method of reimbursement under *managed care* plans where professional providers receive a fixed fee per member per month for each of the plan's enrollees who have selected them as their primary care physician.

Cash Flow   The actual results of practice operations (cash receipts minus disbursements) without consideration of noncash items such as *depreciation* and interest.

Comparative Value   Value based on recent selling prices of area practices similar to the one for sale.

D

Depreciation   The original cost of property, plant, and equipment—sometimes called *fixed assets*—less anticipated *salvage value*, if any. Actual depreciation is the process of allocating the cost of an *asset* to the periods of benefit. Accumulated depreciation is total *depreciation* change on an *asset* since its acquisition.

Designated Health Services   A list of 10 specific entities, as identified by federal legislation, that provide health care services. Referrals to specific services are placed under strict controls for preventing private inurement, private benefit, and other Medicare fraud and abuse violations.

Diagnostic Related Groups (DRGs)   Introduced by Medicare in 1983, DRGs have a fixed fee schedule for 470 categories of illnesses. This schedule determined reimbursement to hospitals for Medicare patients. Replacing the reimbursement system for "reasonable cost," the DRG reimbursement schedules became the standard.

Discounted Cash Flow Valuation (DCF)   Present value of forecasted *cash flow* plus present value of terminal or residual value equals the current value of core operations of the practice.

Discounting   This is a process of projecting present value of the entitlement to receive money in the future, reducing the worth of the dollar by certain percentages for risk and minority interest to its present value.

Discount Rate   The *capitalization rate* applied to convert future income streams to arrive at today's present value.

Discounts   A process of adjusting for risk.

E

EBITDA   Acronym for earnings before interest, taxes, depreciation, and amortization. Various forms of this may include EBIT, EBT, EAT (earnings after taxes).

Equity   Ownership interest.

F

Fair Market Value   Price (value) negotiated at arm's length between a willing buyer and a willing seller, each acting rationally in his or her own self-interest. It may be estimated in the absence of a monetary transaction.

Fee-for-Service (FFS)   A system of payment where payment is made to physicians, hospitals, and other providers based on services rendered to the patient.

G

Going Concern   An ongoing operating business enterprise.

Going Concern Value   The value of a business enterprise that is expected to continue to operate into the future. The intangible elements of going concern value result from factors such as having a trained workforce, an operational plant, and the necessary licenses, systems, and procedures in place.

H

Health Maintenance Organization (HMO)
An organization responsible for providing or arranging the provision of comprehensive health care services on a prepayment basis to voluntarily enrolled persons within a designated population. The providers are aligned and under contract with the plan for a fixed and periodic payment. When an HMO purchases an institution that delivers health care, this model is fully integrated because both financing and delivery of care are provided to the enrolled members.

I

Income Approach to Valuation   Present worth analysis of anticipated future monetary benefits. Estimated future *cash flow* is converted to present value based on an appropriate *discount rate* or rate of return.

Independent Practice Associations (IPAs)
Entities formed by physicians, sometimes with another health care provider, such as a hospital. Generally, they are formed to provide a vehicle for effective contracting with *managed care* purchasers. IPAs contract with HMOs, PPOs, and other managed care companies to provide professional medical services. They differ from group practices in that IPA practices remain independent. Also known as *independent physician associations*.

Intangible Assets   Value based on excess earnings of the practice (ie, earnings greater than

those required to provide a fair return on working capital *assets*). Also called *goodwill*.

Integrated Delivery System (IDS)   Alliances between health care providers including hospitals, sole practitioners, and group practices. Usually, it is designed for providing overall delivery of health care to the patient.

Invested Capital (IC) Method   The sum of *equity* and debt in a business enterprise.

Investment (or Strategic) Value   The value of an asset for specific users reflecting the utility and profitability to an enterprise.

L

Lack of Marketability   The absence of a ready or existing market for the sale of the practice.

Liabilities   Debts due and payable, such as accounts payable, taxes, and notes payable. Current liabilities are those that are due within a short time, usually 1 year.

Liquidation Value   The anticipated revenue from disposing of equipment under a forced or semi-forced condition.

Liquidity   The convertability of an *asset* to cash.

M

Managed Care   A system of financing and providing health care services to a defined group of individuals. Managed care plans provide alliances of providers for the express purpose of containing costs, promoting wellness, and appropriate use of services by its members. Managed care organizations are often HMOs, PPOs, and IPAs.

Management Service Organization (MSO)
An organization formed to provide a cross section of business functions, primarily for administrative management services for physician practices. However, sometimes the primary purpose is for *managed care* contracting. MSOs may also be structured to purchase physician practices and conduct administrative functions for other practices that may not be purchased. Services include accounting, billing, facility management, utilization review, consulting, computer software installation and support, professional fees, marketing, personnel services, etc. Financial arrangements of MSOs are varied. Ownership could include a combination of physicians, hospital, or each of them individually or even include a health care company and insurance company or private investors.

Market Approach to Valuation   Comparative analysis of prices paid for similar *assets* in the marketplace. Value is estimated by using the earnings capitalization multiples derived from sales of comparable medical practices or comparable publicly traded companies.

Market Value What a buyer or seller may expect to obtain for a practice in its related market.

Medicaid A federal program under the Social Security Administration, providing health care benefits to individuals who fall below the poverty level.

Medicare A federal program under the Social Security Administration, providing health insurance benefits to persons older than age 65 and others eligible for Social Security benefits.

Medicare and Medicaid Fraud and Abuse Statute Law specifically outlining the illegality of a health care provider to knowingly and willfully alter, pay, solicit, or receive any remuneration directly or indirectly in return for the referral of a patient for the providing of any services paid for by Medicare or Medicaid.

Minority Interest Ownership of less than 50% control of the ownership of a practice.

P

Physician Hospital Organization (PHO) A health care model where various providers form a network for *managed care* contracting. PHOs are modeled to include at least 1 hospital and a physician affiliation. The physicians may include both primary care and specialty practitioners. Usually, PHOs are separate entities with ownership and/or control divided between hospitals and physicians.

Preferred Provider Organization (PPO) A plan or an organization that contracts with a specific and limited list of independent providers at a discounted fee for service in exchange for a channeled (or directed) patient base.

Price to Earnings (P/E) A typical ratio provided as a benchmark for companies. This is typically used for public companies as the price is readily known. The price to earnings (P/E) ratio is derived by dividing a company's stock price per share by the company's earnings.

Private Benefit Involves an organization, such as a hospital, operating for the benefit of the private interest of designated individuals.

Private Inurement Involves persons who because of their particular relationship with an organization have an opportunity to control or influence activities.

Private Inurement and Private Benefits Under Section 501(c)(3) of the Internal Revenue Code, to qualify for tax-exempt status, a health care organization must not violate *private benefit* and *private inurement* rules. This includes income or *assets*

to be transferred to or for the benefit of any member, officer, or other insider (eg, a physician) with whom it is affiliated.

Proprietorship A privately owned business.

R

Replacement Cost The cost of a duplicate or equally viable substitute.

Reproduction Cost The cost of producing or constructing a new and identical replacement to the *asset*.

Restrictive Covenant An agreement (normally within the context of an employment or services contract) that restricts competition in that particular specialty. In a medical practice, it covers a physician who is agreeing not to compete in the geographical area after the sale or after leaving its employment. Also known as *noncompetition agreements*.

S

Salvage Value For accounting purposes, the estimated value of a depreciable *asset* at the end of its useful life.

Section 501(c)(3) Internal Revenue Code The code section that provides an exemption from federal income tax for not-for-profit organizations formed for charitable or community services.

Single or Multi-Specialty Group Practice Practices consisting of at least 2 physicians with the same or different medical specialties, who typically share office space and other operating expenses.

Sole Proprietorship A business owned by a single individual.

Stark Legislation Named for Congressman Forney "Pete" Stark (D), California, who previously chaired the House committee that addressed Medicare fraud and abuse violations. This legislation—typically called Stark I, II, and III—has specifically set guidelines for such violations.

T

Tangible Assets Property that can be specifically identified and is physical in nature (eg, equipment, land, cash, accounts receivable, buildings).

U

Useful (Service) Life Refers to the period of expected usefulness of a tangible asset in the practice.

W

Weighted Average Cost of Capital (WACC) A method for determining the valuation of the invested capital (IC), ie, debt plus equity.

Page numbers in **bold** represent figures or tables.

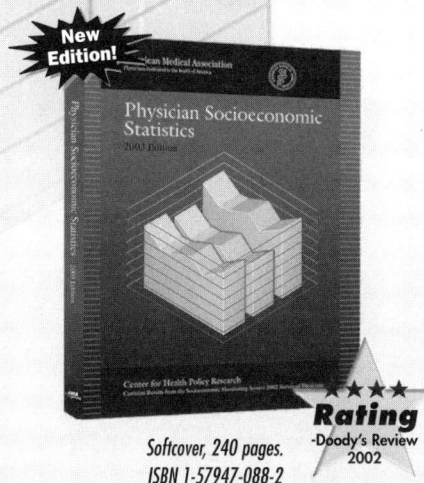